Bytes and Beginnings

Inside the Mind of a Tech Entrepreneur

Andrei Mituca

DEDICATION

To my parents, who planted the seeds of love, resilience, and curiosity within me,

To my brother, my earliest confidant, and lifelong friend, always challenging me to grow,

To my wife, the love of my life, who walks hand in hand with me on this wondrous journey.

To my two boys, who fill my days with joy and wonder, and inspire me to be the best version of myself.

CONTENTS

December 2020 – January 2021

Bytes and Beginnings

1.
THE LEAP FROM CORPORATE TO STARTUP

Every great adventure begins with a single decision. You spend countless days and nights weighing the pros and cons of the choice ahead, even though deep down, you already know what you truly desire. It's your intuition, your inner voice, or the subtle signs from the universe that you attempt to rationalize with your logical mind, justifying a decision you've already made. Should you go left or right, choose red or blue, opt for up or down? Nobody can truly know until they embark on the chosen path. Making the decision often holds more significance than the choice itself as you set off on a new journey. Once you've made the decision, embrace it wholeheartedly, for it's a unique opportunity to learn and achieve more than you ever thought possible.

It was the end of June in 2015 when I made the decision to leave behind the ordinary world with all its conveniences and embark on an entrepreneurial journey. The ordinary world is the environment approved by mainstream society, where success is measured by predefined metrics, and individuals are ranked and evaluated accordingly. There's immense pressure, both internal and external, from peers, family, and societal norms to conform to these rules. In the pursuit of achieving high rankings, one often ends up pursuing goals that aren't truly their own, losing sight of their personal aspirations and happiness. It's the easier path to follow because decisions are made for you, sparing you the effort of thinking and planning. It suits many who achieve more than they initially imagined.

The alternative path is guided by an irresistible urge for risk-taking, by setting your own success metrics, and refusing to compromise your dreams for the sake of security. It's a conscious decision that requires dedication and preparation because success favors those who are prepared to embrace it. On my last day in the corporate world, bidding farewell to colleagues and the comfort of benefits, I stepped outside the building, leaving the safety of my badge behind. It was a new sensation, hearing the door close without the assurance that it would open for me again. It was the scent of freedom mixed with the excitement and anxiety of the unknown. On that day, I was optimistic and confident, fueled by the belief that this was the right choice for a worthwhile adventure.

Some people are driven by faith, while others are fueled by hope. Faith and hope are intertwined yet distinct concepts. Faith is a profound belief and confidence in something that drives you to act. Hope, on the other hand, is the feeling of anticipation and desire for a specific outcome. As I sit in my living room, I hope that one day I will complete a marathon. My faith lies in the confidence that my training plan and its execution will ultimately lead me to achieve that marathon goal. Faith is about taking action and trusting that your decisions and progress will bring your dreams to fruition. The marathon represents my goal, and it's my unwavering faith in my training that gives me the confidence that I will one day complete it.

How did I make the decision to leave the corporate world and start my own company? It was an easy choice for me, driven by my personality traits as a risk-taker and someone who rarely settles for less. In the corporate job, I enjoyed the security of a monthly paycheck. My career had a certain predictability, allowing me to plan my income months and even years ahead. However, my character always pushed me to be productive, make the best use of my time, and contribute to society.

While my corporate job did offer some exciting challenges, they were sporadic, and I found myself yearning for more. I thrived when I had to tackle complex problems, often working tirelessly for days on end to find solutions. While the results were always satisfactory to my superiors and clients, the downtime between these challenges couldn't compare to the excitement of those extraordinary moments. Over time, the allure of a regular paycheck started to fade, and I realized that basic needs were easier to satisfy than I had imagined.

Many arguments could have persuaded me to stay: my great boss, the decent salary, or the fact that the work wasn't too difficult. However, I couldn't settle for less.

The hardest part was submitting my resignation and informing my boss about my decision to leave. It was a more challenging emotional battle than I had anticipated. I found myself in a negotiation with myself. But my ambition, faith in myself, and desire to achieve more outside of corporate confines drove me forward. It was a decision to take ownership and be accountable for my actions and outcomes. I couldn't blame office politics, lack of opportunities, or anyone else for my failures. I needed an optimistic, results-oriented mindset and the determination to take action to achieve my goals.

As I heard the door close behind me that afternoon, I felt a sense of empowerment. I noticed the beauty of the natural surroundings, the birds singing, and the lush greenery that I hadn't appreciated before.

In hindsight, I learned that negotiating with oneself is a mistake. It involves compromising on your principles and limits, often for less than you deserve. This can lead to self-blame and dissatisfaction with the outcome, affecting your performance in the long run. Your principles should never be subject to negotiation. Instead, negotiate with external parties, knowing your bottom line and when to compromise. Holding onto your principles is essential to long-term satisfaction and success.

Decision-making is both intriguing and daunting. It varies from person to person, and we all experience both feelings at different times. Decisions are an integral part of life, and our decision-making energy can be likened to a daily reset. Each morning, we start with a certain amount of decision-making energy to spend throughout the day. The energy level can vary from person to person. Every decision we make depletes this energy, and by the end of the day, we might find ourselves irritable when faced with more decisions. Decisions can be categorized into easy and complex ones, with easy decisions consuming less energy and complex decisions requiring more time and effort.

While there's no precise formula for measuring decision-making energy, understanding your limits and when you're reaching a low point can help you make better choices. Experimentation and observation can help establish a reference point for decision energy and energy per decision, simplifying your daily life. Knowing when to stop for the day can also be invaluable in preserving your decision-making capacity.

In this line of thought, you can save mental energy by automating and simplifying tasks whenever possible. Consistently waking up at the same time, having a coordinated set of clothes, and charging your phone in the evening may seem like small things, but over time, these small tasks can add up to a significant effort. These routine tasks need to function smoothly to provide you with the flexibility to make complex decisions.

You will come to understand that there are better times of the day to make decisions. For example, it might not be the best idea to make a career-changing decision after a long, tiring day or when you're emotionally involved or angry. It may seem like a sign of weakness if you can't make a decision on the spot, especially when multiple parties are involved. However, taking some time to sleep on it or going for a long walk can provide you with fresh insights and help you make a more satisfying long-term decision. It takes a lot of willpower to resist the temptation to decide instantly, but in the long run, it's the best thing you can do for yourself, and others affected by the decision.

When it comes to complex decisions, you often consider their extreme outcomes—either everything exceeds your wildest expectations, and your start-up becomes a unicorn in a year, or it burns through your entire savings in a few months, leaving you without a workplace or the ability to afford rent. Emotional biases often creep into the decision-making process, causing you to seek evidence that supports your ideas while disregarding opposing views. Stepping back, you'll realize that the likelihood of either extreme happening is very low. It's more probable that you'll end up somewhere in between, somewhere closer to the average of the best and worst-case scenarios. Recognizing this fact can help reduce the emotional intensity of your decisions, preventing overconfidence and unnecessary drama and enabling you to make satisfying decisions more quickly. Making decisions faster doesn't just benefit the immediate decision; it also frees up your time and energy, allowing you to focus on what you love instead of endlessly debating pros and cons.

The decision-making process is an art, and you are the artist. It's subjective, inexplicable, random, and irrational. No matter how much research you do or how many facts you gather, personal bias will always play a role. This subjectivity is what makes your decision-making unique and personal—it's your signature. Even top managers who claim to make objective, data-driven decisions have some level of subjectivity. This subjectivity can be obvious, like a personal preference, or hidden in a consultant-prepared presentation, based on an analyst's subjective market estimation. A fully rational, objective decision would imply that you don't care about the decisions or their outcomes, which is rarely the case. There can be many vertical hierarchies and horizontal layers, like a circle of friends, to help diffuse the pressure of a single decision. Large corporations have the luxury of multiple departments and decision-making layers, which reduces pressure on top management. However, young start-ups don't have this luxury, and the pressure falls heavily on the founding team. The scale of the decisions may differ greatly between small and large organizations, but ultimately, whether you must let go of one or a thousand employees, it's still a challenging decision. The emotional weight may be higher when it affects a larger number, but it's still one decision, not a thousand individual ones. In any circumstance, you want to ensure that you make the right decision.

Some decisions will turn out well, while others will prove to be wrong. Making a wrong decision is not inherently bad, as long as you recognize it and acknowledge it as such. Recognizing a poor decision gives you the opportunity to act and rectify it. Choosing not to make a decision allows external factors to make the decision for you, potentially against your preferences. In such cases, you have limited control over enjoying the benefits of a good decision or correcting the consequences of a bad one. The sum of all the decisions you make throughout your life will guide you along your own unique and irreproducible path. You must find joy in this path because it belongs to you and only you. Through your choices, you can determine your direction at the crossroads of options or allow circumstances to guide you in different directions at different times.

In the entrepreneurial journey I've chosen, the pressure to make the right decisions is immense. Even before embarking on this path, we set very high expectations for ourselves and our team regarding what we aim to achieve. Additionally, there are external expectations from our partners, investors, customers, and team members. These external expectations can sometimes conflict with one another and even with our own, potentially appearing unrealistic. These situations are quite common and require a keen awareness to identify them and not allow distractions.

To navigate through these challenges, it's crucial to distinguish between the signals and the distracting noise in the messages we receive. This skill isn't taught in school or learned from a playbook but rather acquired through practice and experience. Being adept at separating signal from noise should become second nature, making our daily endeavors smoother and less mentally taxing.

For instance, consider a scenario where we have a meeting with a potential customer who seems extremely enthusiastic about our product. They express great interest in integrating it into their processes, discuss pricing, and give us the impression that a contract is imminent. However, as time passes, delays and excuses begin to emerge, and the communication dwindles until it ceases altogether. Such experiences can be disheartening, but they teach us to read between the lines and recognize when a sales discussion is merely superficial.

On the other hand, there's a different scenario with a prospect who appears highly skeptical during our product demonstration. They question the functionality and maturity of our product at every turn, leaving us feeling exhausted and aware of the work required to improve it. Weeks go by without any communication, and just when we least expect it, we receive a message saying our product is on the shortlist for a final decision. This unexpected turn of events sparks new hope.

The key difference between these scenarios lies in the nature of the partner we were dealing with. The former may have lacked decision-making authority and was merely offering superficial approval, potentially indicating a lack of ownership within their company's processes. The latter, however, seems to be a decision-maker who thoroughly understands their company's operations and has precise questions about our product's features. Even if the sale doesn't go through, the detailed questions we receive contribute to a better understanding of customer needs and help prioritize future improvements.

Over time, we learn to adjust our expectations based on the character and experience of the other party involved. A negative impression can sometimes be more valuable to our company than constant approval. While constant approval may be a superficial "yes" that doesn't offer substantial insights, a sincere "no" often provides valuable information for improvement. The superficial "yes" might boost our ego momentarily, confirming existing assumptions, but it lacks substance and nutritional value, leaving us hungry for genuine feedback and growth.

As a founder, it's crucial to stay focused on what truly matters and filter out distractions. Over time, you'll get better at distinguishing between important and unimportant things, which will help your company thrive. When you embark on your entrepreneurial journey, you make a conscious decision to be the decision-maker. You're responsible for your own success, and as your company grows, you become the decision-maker for your team as well. You'll develop the skill to recognize when others are also decision-makers. You can tell by the depth and precision of their questions; these experts in their fields will stand out. Focus on connecting with decision-makers because they can save you valuable time.

Avoid getting caught up in lengthy discussions with people who aren't your target audience or decision-makers. Adjust your pitch accordingly or delegate such tasks to others as training opportunities. A brief conversation with a decision-maker who shares your interests can offer crucial insights to guide your product and company towards success.

Time is both your best friend and your worst enemy when making decisions, especially when you don't have a clear deadline. It's tempting to procrastinate by collecting pros and cons or waiting for circumstances to change. While some procrastination can be beneficial, like waiting for more information or observing the market, it rarely provides a significant long-term advantage. Gathering information is essential, but it must come from reliable sources and have a time limit. Successful startup founders often make decisions with incomplete information. Waiting until you have 90% of the data is too late; your competitors and the market will have moved on. Aim for around 70% of the available information to make a decision quickly.

It's a luxury to get everything right on the first try as a founder. Embrace the motto "Fail Fast, Fail Often" as it underscores the importance of timing. Think of your journey as filling two bags: one labeled "luck," which starts full, and another labeled "experience," which begins empty. Your goal is to fill the "experience" bag through decisions and actions before the "luck" bag runs empty. Focus on what truly matters and make informed decisions with the information you have, even if it's incomplete. Take responsibility for your achievements and avoid seeking excuses. Success is self-sustaining and doesn't require excuses.

Leaving the corporate world behind signifies your commitment to achieving high success. This newfound purpose gives you the motivation to wake up every morning with passion. At the end of each day, you should feel satisfied with your decisions and proud of pushing your limits. I experienced this excitement when I left my corporate job in September and booked a flight to Toulouse to start my entrepreneurial journey. My excitement had been building since June when I decided to join a startup with my partners. It kept me going, and I transitioned from my corporate job to the startup within a day. I worked tirelessly without a vacation, eagerly anticipating my flight to our new office in Toulouse at 6:00 a.m. the next morning.

During that time, I didn't think about the risks I was taking. I was so captivated by the idea behind the startup that the material world and its attractions were fading away. I was moving to a country I only knew for its food and wines, to a city I had visited briefly on business trips, and into a shared apartment I hadn't seen before. My mind was filled with excitement about all the new experiences I was about to have. The curiosity of discovering a new culture, meeting new people, exploring new places, making new friends, and learning a new language was overwhelming. I was confident that this was the right decision, and I believed it would be an incredible journey.

I'm someone who likes to get things done, whether it's small tasks like doing the dishes or embarking on exciting travel adventures. Moving to Toulouse was an opportunity for me to make things happen. I was enthusiastic about developing the product, growing the business, and building a reputable company from scratch. The flight symbolized my commitment to leaving behind my previous professional life, and it was a challenging but necessary step. Once I stepped out of the corporate world, I knew there was no turning back. I had to find my way and make this new path work. This commitment was important not only for me but also for my partners. Burning all bridges to the past showed my dedication to the company's success. It meant that I had no fallback plan if things got tough – no returning to my old employer. It's tempting to consider going back, but it's the wrong mindset. As the face of the company to partners and employees, you must lead by example, exuding confidence and faith. Dwelling on the past will only hinder your progress and cause you to miss out on new opportunities. People with passion and a drive to accomplish are rare, and you should take pride in being one of them, making the community proud to have you as a member.

Now, let's discuss the topic of changing one's mind. This issue often arises in decision-making, especially for seemingly trivial matters like choosing between green and blue buttons. Changing a button's color may have a small impact, and developers can easily make such changes. However, if this happens frequently, it can significantly harm your team's perception of your managerial skills. They may see you as inconsistent and prone to changing your mind, which can demotivate them. Why put in the effort to do something well if it's likely to change later in the day? This mindset leads to minimal effort and waiting for changes, resulting in an underperforming team and lower-quality work. If an undecided leader doesn't provide the expected changes, the product ends up mediocre.

Changing one's mind is sometimes the right thing to do, especially when correcting a bad decision. It can have positive outcomes, as long as it's based on solid evidence and not abused. However, stubbornly sticking to a bad decision or changing your mind too frequently are both detrimental. The key is to base decisions on relevant metrics. For example, if data shows that a blue button has a 50% higher click rate than a green button, it makes sense to change all buttons to blue. When decisions are supported by such metrics, there's usually no need for debate within the team.

The previous example of button colors illustrates how a leader can avoid the need to change their mind. Instead of deciding whether the buttons should be green or blue, one can opt to gather information on which color is preferred by customers. There are various tools and processes available to help you gather insights for such binary decisions. This approach not only reflects positively on your character and decision-making style but also emphasizes that customer satisfaction and the company's best interests are your top priorities. It also communicates that mandatory changes are based on measurable data and are in the product's best interest.

In the examples above, you've read about a top-down decision-making process, where as a manager, you have to make and communicate decisions to your peers. This isn't contradictory to the highly promoted "flat hierarchy" models often seen in startup ecosystems. In these flat hierarchies, communication channels are open across all functions, and all team members have the freedom to express their views on company matters. As a founder, you have a moral obligation to listen to these inputs.

Here are a few different scenarios related to team involvement in the decision-making process:

1. The decision is obvious, and the entire team is on board. In this case, everyone is happy, understands the decision, and can work together toward the common goal.

2. The decision is almost obvious, and the team agrees, but it's a risky decision with potential implications for the company. Even though the decision is clear, someone must take ownership and support the team's choice. This ensures that the decision is executed with confidence.

3. The team has diligently prepared metrics for a decision, and the data clearly points in a specific direction. However, as a leader, you may not be experienced in that particular domain. In such cases, if the team has already reached a decision, it's often best to accept their recommendation rather than making them spend unnecessary time convincing you.

Recognizing and addressing a bad decision early is crucial. If your team can independently make decisions, it's a testament to your previous decision to hire a high-quality team. Supporting their decisions demonstrates your commitment to your team and your own decision-making standards. Remember, a good decision today can simplify your future work significantly.

As a professional or entrepreneur, there will be times when you can't fully explain your decision-making process to the team. Good communication skills and your team's trust are essential in such situations. Occasionally, you may need to make decisions against the team's wishes, but always in the best interest of the company or product. Understand that you can't make everyone happy simultaneously, but as long as you're content with your decisions and remain true to your principles, you can justify them to both supporters and opponents. Avoid negotiating against yourself, as it often leads to disappointment.

The decisions you make define your unique path toward individual success. Succeeding at a thriving company is much easier than at an unsuccessful one, but it's impossible to predict a company's fate at its founding. Your role as a founder is to establish sound principles, stick to them, and strive to make good decisions. Many external factors can influence a young company's success or failure, but it's your team's responsibility to identify and capitalize on opportunities that will shape your entrepreneurial journey.

2.
THE TRANSFORMATIVE POWER OF MENTORS

The decision to start your own company or take on a new role at a different company, to embark on an adventure with an unknown outcome, or anything that takes you out of your comfort zone is a testament to your strong-willed nature. It reflects your strong desire to do something significant and your willingness to take action. The fear of not trying often outweighs the fear of failing. You've decided to leave behind the ordinary world, where daily routines have been in place for a long time, and do something different. Maybe you've been hearing the call to adventure from your inner voice for a while but never had the courage to take the leap. Perhaps you've had a long internal debate, trying to convince yourself of the benefits of your old routine in the ordinary world. Finally, you've listened to that inner voice, accepting the call to adventure.

Taking this call to adventure may seem like a recent decision, but the seeds for it may have been planted long ago. The people you've surrounded yourself with, your colleagues, managers, and friends, may have contributed small pieces of information over time, helping those seeds grow into mature ideas. These individuals, whom you consider friends and role models, have engaged you in valuable discussions and learning opportunities, even if they weren't officially designated as coaches or mentors. You may not have realized the significance of these interactions or how important they were for your future self. Unbeknownst to you, they provided the nourishment and encouragement needed for you to make the courageous decision to venture into the unknown. At best, you were consciously seeking out smart, competent, and friendly people, hoping that their wisdom would benefit you in the future. It may have been luck or mere coincidence that led you to such a fortunate environment.

I had a similar experience when I had the privilege of working with RIF and AdVa. At the time, I was too young to fully appreciate the lessons they taught me. Sometimes, I was too arrogant and inexperienced to see the broader implications of their guidance, focusing only on short-term gains. Nevertheless, there were instances when I was open and eager to learn, and those lessons have stayed with me over the years. It was only in hindsight, as I progressed on my journey, that I realized the profound influence these individuals had on me and, consequently, on my company.

RIF was my colleague during my first job as a software engineer. Our office was in a unique location, sandwiched between a model agency and a speaker reseller. While we had a common manager, I regarded RIF as the authority on all technical matters and considered him a role model. I admired his character—a kind, calm person with impeccable logic and a positive attitude. Beyond my regular duties, which didn't overlap with RIF's responsibilities, I learned from him about web technologies and frameworks. RIF was a software developer at heart, with a wealth of experience and an insatiable curiosity. He often introduced me to new technologies, better approaches to writing code, and simplifying complex code. I learned from him the art of implementing features with simplicity, which, to me, meant avoiding unnecessary complexity and achieving elegant, easy-to-understand code. I also picked up Python, Objective C, and a bit of Go through his guidance. Learning with him was always a pleasure because of his relaxed, clear way of explaining complex concepts. While I wasn't the ideal student, some of his teachings stayed with me. Learning about Web2Py and the Django framework, as well as Python, had a significant impact on my decisions when I assumed the role of a technical co-founder in a startup. We still keep in touch, and our interactions continue to motivate me with his positive attitude and solution-oriented mindset. From one of our meetings, I recall a song he recommended, "I Can See Clearly Now" by Johnny Nash. I've played that song repeatedly when faced with difficult decisions or when solutions were elusive. Listening to the song and adopting a positive attitude, envisioning clear skies all around, has consistently helped me maintain a constructive mindset and find the right solutions. It became a valuable fallback solution in many situations later on.

AdVa was my manager during the gap year between my bachelor's and master's studies in Munich. I had initially connected with AdVa while searching for a job in Timisoara, where I ultimately chose to work with RIF. It was quite an interesting turn of events that we ended up working together in Munich. I had the privilege of learning a lot from him, and I owe him and his wife my gratitude, although I may not have always expressed it as well as I should have.

AdVa is an incredibly ambitious and hardworking individual with tremendous willpower. He possessed a level of energy and determination that I had never encountered before. When we first met, he was the first person I knew who had run a marathon, and he had completed many of them without extensive training. It was sheer willpower and determination that defined his character. He once shared a story with me about how he was unsure if he could finish a mountain marathon, so he ran the same course a week before the race just to ensure he could do it. Another time, shortly after I started working with him, he ran a marathon during the day, only for us to drive more than 1200 kilometers overnight and arrive at the office the next morning for a regular workday.

There are numerous stories of our business trips throughout Germany, France, the UK, and South Korea. AdVa taught me the importance of seizing the moment, making the most of every experience, and truly appreciating the beauty of life. I learned that with determination and a strong will, one can push physical boundaries beyond what they ever thought possible. AdVa also had a positive and solution-oriented mindset that I greatly admired. He always saw the good in others and did his best to fulfill their requests.

What I learned from AdVa was not just about technical skills but also about the power of determination and the belief that anything is possible. It reinforced the idea that code is essentially text – something we write to instruct machines. Therefore, there is no bug that cannot be fixed or feature that cannot be implemented.

My time with RIF and AdVa provided both technical and social training. They both had a positive, solution-oriented mindset, a trait I now proudly call my own and which has proven invaluable in my entrepreneurial journey. It's interesting to note that both RIF and AdVa decided to become self-employed shortly after I left the companies we worked for together. I stayed in contact with both of them as they embarked on their individual journeys in the professional world. Later on, I realized this coincidence and how it might have unconsciously influenced my own desire to become an entrepreneur.

Sometimes, your mentorship journey may have already started without you realizing it or without any formal acknowledgment. It could be a colleague or manager whom you deeply respect for their technical or social skills, and they are willing to share their knowledge with you. It's crucial to accept their guidance, enjoy their company, and always remain open to learning. As a founder, you will rely on mentors to provide you with direction on your journey. You may not always understand how their information is relevant, but you never know when it might prove invaluable. You must appreciate every learning opportunity, every lesson, every piece of advice you receive and accumulate that knowledge.

The challenges faced by founders are both technical and personal, and they are intertwined. Sometimes, solving a personal problem can lead to insights into technical challenges. Learning from the experiences of your mentors, both formal and informal, is essential. What you've achieved so far is a result of your past experiences and knowledge. To achieve something greater and surpass your previous accomplishments, you must be willing to try different approaches. A mentor who believes unconditionally in your abilities, even when you or others doubt them, is an invaluable asset for any entrepreneur. The principles and values your mentors represent are what you will remember long after you've forgotten specific lessons. A mentor will share their experiences for you to build upon but will also provide constructive feedback and criticism when needed. It's up to you to accept this feedback and build a relationship of trust and confidence, using it for your own growth. In a mentor, you can find guidance and validation, which will prepare you to face extraordinary challenges, for these challenges do not wait for you to be ready; they arrive when they are due.

When embarking on the journey of creating a startup, the initial question that arises is, "Where do I begin?" With the rise of the startup trend, many universities now offer various courses and programs to support aspiring founders. These programs are readily accessible to students and provide valuable guidance to help them kickstart their ventures. Additionally, private enterprises offer numerous programs and resources to non-students. There is also a wealth of online material on entrepreneurship, and with some filtering, you can find high-quality information.

Among the most established programs that aid startups in their early stages are incubators and accelerators. These programs typically run for a predetermined period, follow varying schedules, and culminate in a demo day. During this grand finale, participants have the opportunity to showcase their products or services to a select group of investors and customers. Incubators and accelerators may also offer financial support in the form of grants or equity exchange. What these programs have in common is their commitment to providing coaching and mentoring to founders. Typically, a coach is assigned to each team or individual, closely monitoring project progress.

For a coaching relationship to be effective, it must be a two-way exchange. The coach should be willing to share their knowledge, while the coachee must be open to receiving this knowledge. The coach should have confidence in their experience, be a sincere communicator, and be content with their role and expertise. They should also exude confidence and respect towards their teams. Coachees must recognize the value of their coach and actively seek the right fit. If the coaching relationship is unproductive, both parties should be willing to consider a change for the benefit of all involved. Finding the right coach is crucial, as it can potentially lead to a long-term, fruitful relationship.

More experienced incubators and accelerators have access to a larger pool of coaches, making it easier to find a suitable match. Newer incubators may be better suited for businesses exploring innovative models and technologies. It's vital not to settle for less and to take the initiative to find the right coach. Having a coach just for the sake of it, without valuing their input, is counterproductive and a missed opportunity.

It's important to note that what an incubator or accelerator labels as a coach may, in some cases, be a project manager guiding your company through a structured process defined by the organization. In such instances, clear expectations should be set. Regardless, an incubator offers numerous facilities and incentives, and it's in your best interest to be aware and make wise use of them.

In the previous paragraphs, I have used the terms "mentor" and "coach" somewhat interchangeably. The concepts of mentoring and coaching are relatively new, and their definitions can be somewhat blurry. Experts have various and sometimes conflicting definitions for these terms. How I prefer to distinguish them is by viewing mentoring as an informal knowledge transfer process from experienced individuals to less experienced ones, while coaching is a more structured consulting approach where two people work on a particular topic without providing a clear solution. It is the responsibility of the coachee to identify the right solution after the consultation. Both coaching and mentoring are valuable tools for personal development. In this sense, it's more important to acknowledge and accept a mentor or coach than to get caught up in the exact title. Having a mentor or coach signifies maturity in your leadership journey, demonstrating your willingness to learn, self-awareness, and a strong interest in continuous learning.

In my own entrepreneurial experience, we began our startup journey with the incubator of a prominent Munich university. The incubator provided us with a coach, free office space, a small amount of financial aid, and access to their network. At that stage, our project was in its infancy, just beginning to develop the first prototype. The incubator had strong industry connections relevant to our startup, granting us access to local events and valuable feedback on our business plan. Our office space was shared with other companies at similar developmental stages, offering opportunities for collaboration and discussions on relevant topics. Networking was crucial in these early stages to identify experts and potential customers, gathering their feedback on our product and business model. In many ways, an incubator acts as a seal of approval for a startup, validating the project, the idea, and the team. The more prestigious the incubator, the greater the confidence it instills in potential customers, partners, and investors, helping to establish trust.

Our time in the Munich incubator was overshadowed by the unexpected acceptance into the Airbus incubator. Against all odds and expectations, our project was chosen as part of the first cohort. It felt like a stroke of luck, as our chances of acceptance were statistically around 3%. We were immensely proud of this achievement and headed to Toulouse with high spirits. Little did we know that this would mark the beginning of a long-lasting collaboration with the aircraft manufacturer, extending well beyond the initial six months of incubation. Being allowed to use the Airbus BizLab logo on our slides was a significant validation, demonstrating the doors that open when you have such a reputable backer supporting your venture.

In the beginning, we were among the first group of startups accepted into the accelerator program. At that time, the processes and structures were still being established. This phase was a steep learning curve for both us, the startups, and the accelerator itself as we all worked together to get things right. What united us was our strong desire to learn and succeed.

It's important to note that the accelerator didn't provide any financial support to our company. Instead, they offered the valuable resources of their umbrella company, a supportive network, and office space. However, our motivation was unwaveringly high. During the program, we received coaching on various topics relevant to our project. Our coaches were dedicated to our success and used their expertise to support us. They often tapped into their internal network to connect us with industry experts who could provide input and feedback on our product.

It was during this period that our project experienced significant growth, and as founders, we worked tirelessly to address various challenges. Being part of the BizLab accelerator was a pivotal moment in our startup's history, opening up new opportunities. Having the backing of BizLab was a strong endorsement of our project, giving us the confidence to approach partners for collaborations under the aircraft manufacturer's umbrella.

Our time in BizLab was instrumental in achieving our project's highest successes. It's a prime example of seizing the moment and making the most of an opportunity. The partnerships we established during this period turned out to be a unique selling point for our project in the years that followed. The extensive network we built during our stay remained unmatched by our competitors. Our official coaches played a significant role in establishing connections within the company, while our determination to succeed drove our growth. We continued our association with BizLab for a few more years before eventually moving on.

Networking is a crucial factor in the success of a young company. The size and quality of your network matter significantly. Building a strong network through mentors, incubators, and accelerators is a solid foundation for making valuable industry contacts and establishing key relationships.

A high-quality network with a positive, solution-oriented mindset can influence your own thinking and motivation positively. Having the right contacts is essential because they can be your lifeline in challenging situations. Timely advice from the right person can save you a lot of time and stress. Therefore, it's not just about having a broad network but about cultivating a deep and trustworthy network of contacts you can rely on when needed.

You can create your own "mastermind" group from this carefully selected network of trusted individuals. These are people you respect for their values, principles, and expertise, considering them role models in their fields. They don't need to know each other or communicate directly; their common link is you. Your mastermind group becomes an extension of your own capabilities, providing you with a reliable source of confidence and guidance when you face challenges.

As an entrepreneur, manager, or simply a person, you can't possibly know everything. Acknowledging this fact is perfectly fine, but it's your responsibility to find trustworthy sources for high-quality information when needed. You have control over the quality of the sources and information you seek. Start small, such as by choosing reliable magazines or sources of information to ensure you're making well-informed decisions.

Building your mastermind, determining its size, and selecting its members are entirely within your control. It's crucial to prioritize creating your own mastermind as soon as possible. It will empower you and provide the confidence you need when facing critical decisions. Having a mastermind can be the difference between achieving greatness and extraordinary success.

In life, as in networking, you can't please everyone at once. The same holds true for the people you connect and network with. Some will support your ideas, others will be indifferent or fail to understand your work and efforts, and a few may even feel threatened by you. These individuals, although seemingly harmless, can have a significant negative impact on your progress.

The six degrees of separation rule suggests that any two people worldwide can be introduced to each other within six steps. This implies that in the entrepreneurial world, the social distance among entrepreneurs, investors, and both is significantly less than six. In my experience in the industry my startup was part of, I'd estimate our social distance was at most three, and after five years, it dropped to one or two for most decision-makers. With such close proximity, actions are closely observed and can be subject to scrutiny, even unofficially, by others.

However, it's not in your best interest to focus on competition or to be overly concerned about what others think of your actions. If you're acting based on your expertise and the input of your trusted advisors, you don't need to justify yourself to anyone. The group of people mentioned earlier—those who don't believe in or feel threatened by you—shouldn't be your primary focus, but they can still pose a challenge to your growth.

These individuals may include:

- Influential and highly respected experts in the industry who have their own trusted advisors. If negative feedback about your project reaches them, collaborations might not go as planned. Unfortunately, you often won't receive a clear explanation for the sudden end of a project.
- Individuals or small groups who feel threatened by your work, especially if they have positional power

within an organization that is a key customer. They may find reasons to justify why collaborating with you is a bad idea, such as it being too expensive or someone else being a better fit. Such actions are typically driven by ego and the fear that your work might undermine theirs.

These two types of individuals are usually not your direct competitors, as they understand the effort required to reach your stage. True competitors engage in a fair, equal, and continuous effort to win over customers and investors, fostering constructive competition that benefits the industry and customers.

Dealing with these negative influences in your network involves addressing dormant conflicts. Ignoring them won't benefit anyone. Instead, actively seek communication and try to understand each other's perspectives. This may not lead to friendship but can foster mutual respect and understanding. It's okay to agree to disagree as long as disagreements are transparent and based on solid facts. Often, silent conflicts arise from misunderstandings or information gaps. Actively communicating and clarifying topics is a good start to peaceful coexistence.

Let me share a real-life scenario to illustrate how such situations can arise. Some years ago, we were in negotiations with a potential client for a significant project. Since it was a major customer, the negotiations took a while to involve all the necessary parties and define the project's scope.

During the initial phase, we were introduced to an internal stakeholder who was launching an in-house software project that partially overlapped with our offering. To clarify, their project covered a specific aspect but required manual intervention. In contrast, our software already provided more comprehensive functionality, although it didn't address the specific areas of their project. So, it seemed logical for both parties to collaborate, benefiting our customers and potential new ones. Surprisingly, no cooperation or further communication occurred.

Years passed, and neither side discussed the matter further. Each pursued their separate paths, and projects continued to grow. Eventually, in a collaboration involving our company and a large corporation with whom we had negotiated earlier, a new project emerged. This time, a different project manager from a different country led the effort, with no involvement from the internal stakeholder we had met years before.

The project progressed smoothly, with excellent teamwork, efficient communication, and prompt issue resolution. External stakeholders were pleased with the results, and discussions began to expand the project's reach across borders. All parties were satisfied as the project's hard work started to pay off. As discussions expanded, the project scope needed to cover new use cases and refine existing functionality.

In the late stages of the project, the same internal manager we had met years ago, working on the internal software initiative, became interested in our ongoing project. As soon as he joined, questions arose about the project's approach and why they should pay for functionality when his project could provide something similar. Unfortunately, this led to frustration among the project manager and the team. Their motivation dwindled, and the external stakeholders were only interested in results, not internal politics. The project came to a halt and was eventually canceled, causing negative consequences for the company.

So, why is this story relevant to the mentorship chapter? It's a compelling story because it highlights human behavior. The internal manager may have acted out of self-interest and self-preservation to promote his own project, which is natural. However, it was this self-centered perspective that ultimately caused the project's failure. Instead of focusing on collective success, he may have been concerned that we would expand our software at the expense of his project. This could have been projection—seeing our company as a mirror of his own desires and actions. People often react based on their egos, seeking validation for their actions, and this can be a destructive force, blinding them to the bigger picture.

The project's downfall resulted from this ego-driven behavior, leading to financial losses and reputational damage for the large corporation where the manager worked. The alternative is to channel constructive energy towards benefiting the group. Instead of saying, "I can do this better," the manager could have offered, "I have features that could significantly enhance the project's outcomes." This would have demonstrated a constructive focus on delivering the best possible results.

You must be able to distinguish between people driven by ego and those who genuinely want to contribute to something greater. When building your circle of mentors, choose individuals who possess constructive energy. Carefully select them because each one will, over time and through discussions, plant a seemingly insignificant seed in your mind.

Think of your mind as fertile soil, providing the necessary environment and nutrients for that small seed to flourish. From this seemingly powerless seed, a robust, tall tree can grow, or it might become a weed. These ideas and relationships must be nurtured or pruned early to ensure that only those aligning with your ultimate goal are cultivated. This selection process demands energy, and it's easier to control what type of seeds are sown into your mind than to clean up the soil later.

It's equally important to maintain an open mind, allowing new ideas and mentorship to take root. No mentor or coach can benefit you if you aren't receptive to their guidance. Be willing to absorb their knowledge through your own unique perspective. As soon as you can envision something, you have the potential to grow it into a successful, scalable product.

In this section, we've discussed mentors, coaches, incubators, and accelerators. Before you have these formal sources of support, you have your family and friends. They stand by your side from the very beginning of your entrepreneurial journey. They invest countless hours listening to your vision of success and offer encouragement when things don't go as planned. It's easy to take their presence and support for granted, but take a moment to appreciate the gift of family and friends.

Every family and relationship is unique, making it challenging to describe them comprehensively. However, the solidarity and trust that exist within these relationships are undeniable. Often, they assist you simply by lending an ear. While they may not influence your decisions (and it's usually best that they don't), sharing your ideas out loud allows you to test your feelings and seek confirmation. You want to be heard and feel like you belong to a group where your role is essential.

This sense of inclusion is vital because entrepreneurship can be a lonely journey. You make many decisions individually and in consultation with your mastermind group. You must be accountable for your actions in front of your team and business stakeholders.

3.
IF YOU CAN THINK IT, YOU CAN DO IT

One can never conquer the summit of Mount Everest without first having the thought of doing so. This might seem obvious, but the same principle applies to many other aspects of life. Whether it's desiring a house with a pool, owning a convertible car, or running a marathon, it all begins with a genuine desire. You must say to yourself, "I will conquer Mount Everest! I will own a house with a pool! I will have a convertible car! I will run a marathon!" Simply observing someone else's achievements, like saying, "That person is lucky to have conquered Mount Everest," isn't enough. Your desire must be expressed as a strong statement of your own wishes. Thinking is the first step toward taking action.

This is an encouragement to awaken your creative spirit, to think beyond yourself, and to envision a world that others might not see.

Once you've had the thought, you can imagine and plan for it. Nobody is claiming that achieving your goal will be easy or quick, but the key message is that anything you can think of is attainable. When you think of a goal, you can create a plan with milestones to help you achieve it. For some goals, it's relatively easy to devise a plan, and you can often find valuable information from others who have shared their experiences. For example, consider running a marathon, for which there are numerous free resources available online and in print. After you've thought about running a marathon, you can quickly start training based on a well-structured plan. Surprisingly, a similar situation applies to an expedition to Mount Everest. There are abundant online resources on how to prepare for this adventure of a lifetime. You can find information on how to get ready, what to expect, and the necessary resources to make the expedition possible. Some of the requirements may initially seem insurmountable, but if you stay motivated, solutions to overcome the challenges will become apparent.

You may have never run a kilometer in your life, but you need to run a little over 42 kilometers in just three months. You can start today with 1 kilometer and add a kilometer each day until you gradually build the stamina to complete a marathon. The initial desire is to finish a marathon, but once you achieve that, you can aim to finish first in a marathon race. Similarly, if you've never climbed anything higher than a small hill but want to train for Everest, you can create a plan: start by climbing smaller mountains in your area to build your fitness, train and ascend a few peaks over 6,000 meters to acclimate to high altitudes, and raise the funds needed for the ascent. Each of these individual milestones may seem daunting at first, but you can break them down into smaller, achievable goals and work through them one by one. It may take several years to become the overnight success who conquers Mount Everest.

This is a call to your willpower and your commitment to put in the hard work required to achieve your goals. It's about turning your creative thoughts into actions.

In the two examples mentioned above, planning the implementation phase is relatively straightforward because there are plenty of resources and guidelines available to guide you to success. Many people have achieved what might seem impossible, and it's within your reach to do the same. This is a personal challenge where you are only competing with yourself and your own thoughts. As mentioned in an earlier chapter, negotiating with yourself often leads to failure. Instead, negotiate with a third party—your goal should be to complete the marathon or reach Mount Everest, not to convince yourself that you can do it later, that it's too hard, or that it doesn't make sense, and so on. Once you achieve your goal, you'll gain confidence in your abilities and willpower. You'll dare to dream even bigger and work consistently toward your goals. Dreaming big is essential because running six times seven kilometers is not the same as running a marathon.

Achieving personal goals that have a clear path to completion is relatively straightforward. These goals can boost your self-esteem because they demonstrate your ability to stick to a plan. On the other hand, there are dreams that require a healthy dose of creativity. These dreams are ambitious, challenging the status quo, and pushing the boundaries of what's currently possible. To achieve such dreams, you can't simply follow a training program or rely on other people's experiences. You'll be forging a new path, step by step, with the goal of creating a blueprint for others to follow. One example of such a dream is building and scaling your own startup. While it may not be rocket science, it's akin to someone dreaming of becoming the first commercial visitor to the moon.

These audacious dreams serve as the foundation for creating your vision. Every successful project begins with a well-defined and easily remembered vision that motivates you to get out of bed each morning. The challenge with pursuing visions that haven't been seen before is that you must first create everything in your imagination before making it accessible to others. You have to blaze a trail where there was none before, even when it seems impossible. Remember that conquering Mount Everest was once deemed impossible until Edmund Hillary achieved it. Likewise, powered flight was out of reach until the Wright brothers proved otherwise at Kitty Hawk. It took less than seven years from the time President Kennedy presented the dream of going to the moon to Neil Armstrong's historic moonwalk.

If humanity can reach the moon and harness nuclear energy within such a short span, it's evidence that you can achieve your goals too. It doesn't matter how far-fetched your goals may seem or how much they challenge the accepted worldview. What truly matters is where you direct your focus and determination toward the ultimate goal. Consider the example of stomach ulcers, once thought to be incurable and a result of stress and poor eating habits. However, two scientists dared to think differently, suggesting that stomach ulcers were caused by a bacteria. Despite widespread skepticism, they proved their theory and made the impossible possible by curing the disease. You must remain steadfast in your pursuit of your final goal and work to shape the world as you envision it.

When you envision a new world, describe an innovative process, or share a new idea, you may find that language limitations constrain your ability to communicate effectively. These limitations vary from one language to another, making it challenging to explain something that doesn't yet exist in terms that others can understand. Often, new terms must be coined to describe these novel concepts, or existing words are repurposed with new meanings. It's not uncommon for words once found only in science fiction novels to be adopted by engineers to express their inventions. This cross-pollination of ideas between artists and engineers is mutually beneficial and contributes to societal progress. In a way, the words we use become a standard for evaluating one's ideas. Long after we forget the specific words someone used, we still remember how and why they said it.

When embarking on an unfamiliar journey, whether it's training for a marathon, scaling Mount Everest, or starting your own company, there are typically three phases that everyone experiences.

In the first phase, there's the excitement of beginning something new. It's the curiosity and thrill of venturing into the unknown that motivates you to take on the chosen activity. This phase is familiar to many, especially at the start of each new year when gyms and sports facilities become crowded with enthusiastic individuals pursuing their New Year's resolutions. However, this excitement often fades after a few weeks as fewer people continue their training. It's during this time that you finally get to use the equipment you like, but you also notice others giving up, and you may find yourself making excuses like, "I don't feel well today," "I'll go tomorrow," "It's too crowded," "It's raining outside," or "It's too far away."

These thoughts signal the onset of the second phase of your journey. In this stage, the initial excitement has waned, and you begin to question why you're pursuing this endeavor. You realize how challenging it is compared to the comfort of lounging on the couch, and you start finding reasons why it's not worth continuing. This is when most people give up, as their initial motivation has faded, and they focus on their old routines, which may not have been so bad after all. However, returning to those old routines won't lead to greatness. To endure this second stage, you need a lot of willpower. You must stay focused on the end goal and recognize that overnight success requires years of effort. It's a challenging phase because you must resist the urge to negotiate with yourself and keep moving forward despite the resistance you encounter. The inertia of your old habits will try to pull you back, as inertia is the tendency to do nothing or remain unchanged.

Overcoming this inertia and reaching the point of no return is crucial.

Once you reach the point of no return, inertia starts working in your favor. It will resist any change to your new habits. Through significant willpower, you've conquered the obstacles on your path and established a routine of tackling difficult tasks as part of your daily life. This might include something as simple as making a to-do list every morning or going jogging regardless of the weather. You've formed habits, making these tasks easier to accomplish. You've figured out how to dress appropriately for a run in any weather, how to warm up, and how to prepare your gear. In the world of startups, you've developed habits for thriving in uncertain environments, tackling new challenges every day, and consistently delivering effective solutions. Embracing these new habits has transformed your behavior, marking a significant step toward success. Successful people have the habit of doing what unsuccessful people are often reluctant to do.

You've made a quantum leap toward success by overcoming your inner doubts and channeling your constructive energy into turning your vision into reality. At this point, you've defined your vision through your own creative power. You may have broken barriers and challenged the status quo on your journey, having to be creative multiple times to build new bridges. Understand that things may not always turn out exactly as you imagined. Expectations can be exceeded, but there may also be disappointments. It's important to recognize that positive and negative, good and bad are labels we emotionally attach to events. You have full control over how you choose to label actions and events, even in the face of disappointment, and there's always something to learn from every experience.

The labels we assign to events are products of our imagination and can vary widely from person to person. These labels are often influenced by our past experiences, emotional connections, and how events align with our expectations. For instance, losing $100 on a deal might be seen as a negative outcome by one person, while another person might view it as positive, and vice versa for earning $1000. It's a highly subjective process that depends on our perspective, mindset, and the circumstances at the time.

Past experiences play a significant role in how we label situations. When we've had positive outcomes in the past, we tend to repeat similar actions and avoid those that led to negative results. This approach works well for predictable situations, like not touching a hot object to prevent harm. However, in complex situations with many variables, relying solely on past experiences can be challenging because even a slight change in any of these variables can lead to a different result. Additionally, the meaning we attach to an event can change over time.

Instead of asking "why" something happened in the past, it's often more productive to focus on "how" and "where" to go next in the present.

Here's an example from our startup's early days. We had the opportunity to apply for a non-refundable grant and scholarship during our incubation with a local university. The application process seemed straightforward, and the university, which offered mentoring and consulting, had a near-perfect track record of success with similar applications. Other startups we knew had successfully received the grant, so we were confident in our chances.

However, to our surprise, our application was rejected. This rejection was initially a blow to our motivation because we had counted on this funding to build our first prototype and provide the founders with a one-year scholarship to work full-time on the project. At that moment, the rejection felt extremely negative, and we went to great lengths to understand why it happened and what we could improve.

While waiting for an evaluation of our first submission, we continued working on the project and applied to another accelerator program. Against the odds, we were accepted into the program's first cohort, which was a pleasant surprise. This led us to relocate to a different city and continue developing our project. Through the accelerator's network, we connected with investors and successfully closed our first seed round shortly after.

n the grant application process, we faced several restrictions that initially seemed challenging. First, the company couldn't be officially registered before receiving the funding. This meant we couldn't seek investors or customers without a legal entity. Initially, we viewed the rejection of our application as a setback because it meant we didn't secure the funding or scholarship we hoped for. However, in hindsight, this rejection had a positive aspect. It allowed us to approach investors and register our company, which we couldn't have done otherwise.

Our perception of reality depends on how we label events. These labels shape our expectations, self-evaluation, and reactions. They create an imagined reality in our minds, even though nothing physical has changed. For example, if we label an event as negative, like losing $100, we might become irritable with friends. Conversely, if we label it as positive, such as receiving $100, we might act cheerful and generous.

We have control over how we label events, and these labels influence our reality. By carefully defining your reality and your vision, you shape your environment.

The grant application process required a lot of effort and bureaucracy, leading to feelings of powerlessness and frustration. This contradicted our desire to secure the grant for our startup's success. However, when applying for a corporate accelerator, everything seemed to fall into place effortlessly. Traveling long distances and facing sleep deprivation didn't feel exhausting; it was an exciting adventure. The same project that was rejected for the grant was accepted for the accelerator. Did our unconscious beliefs and desires play a role in this contrasting experience? There's no easy answer, but our labels, such as "hard" and "easy," may have influenced our perceptions.

Experimenting with labeling actions and events can reveal their impact on your reality. For instance, I participated in a pitching competition with confidence, believing I could excel without preparation. This confidence led to a successful performance. You can apply a similar approach to negotiations, whether for salary, car prices, or personal discussions. Visualize a positive outcome, believe in your abilities, and act accordingly, even when success seems unlikely. Practicing this mindset can turn the seemingly impossible into reality, especially on a startup journey.

4.
THE METAMORPHOSIS OF THE CTO IN A MODERN START-UP

In the world of modern startups, one of the early challenges is finding the right person for the role of Chief Technology Officer (CTO). When you browse through startup job listings, you'll notice a significant difference between the number of openings for CTOs compared to Chief Executive Officers (CEOs) or Chief Financial Officers (CFOs). This raises a few questions: Why is it so difficult to find a CTO? And why do we often hear about the CEO's exciting endeavors but rarely about the CTO's contributions?

I have a technical background, having studied at the Technische Universität München, with a focus on computer architectures and IT security. Early in my career, I responded to a job posting on my university's website for a position that intrigued me: "Software Engineer - Co-

Founder." The description was quite vague about the company's vision and maturity, and it listed a wide range of required skills, from security expertise to UX/UI design, 3D geometry optimization, and even knowledge of embedded systems for Raspberry Pi development. Some sentences in the description didn't make much sense.

Despite these challenges, I was drawn to the opportunity. Initially, it was the security aspect that piqued my interest, aligning with my educational background. What kept me engaged was the diversity of tasks that demanded a unique skill set. I saw it as a chance to learn, explore, and experiment in various areas of software engineering. I wasn't deterred by my lack of some advertised skills; instead, I saw it as an opportunity to grow and build something remarkable. The fear of failure was overshadowed by the fear of not trying to build the project from the ground up.

This feeling of excitement is similar when I peruse startup job ads as a technical founding member. Many startups in e-commerce seek web development skills, while others focus on leveraging machine learning algorithms for their business models. What stands out is the promise of the Co-Founder and CTO titles, coupled with detailed technology requirements.

Interestingly, the expectations often paint a picture of a genius hacker living in a dark room, glued to three monitors, coding around the clock. This perception arises from the mix of technologies listed in the job ads, the expected expertise in each area, and the salary expectations. The ideal candidate should be a jack-of-all-trades, cost-effective, and enthusiastic about the CTO title and startup life. But does this portrayal truly resonate with someone immersed in their coding den?

In reality, these positions often require more of a software developer who can build the initial product prototype envisioned by the founders. The technology stack is diverse, and it usually takes a team of developers to meet the ambitious product expectations. Such developers should receive fair compensation, whether in cash or equity. It's crucial to acknowledge that, at this early stage, what the team truly needs is skilled developers rather than dangling fancy titles and decision-making power as bait. An alternative is hiring an external development agency, but this has its drawbacks: it requires cash payments, and the startup loses the appeal of having a CTO as a founding member when pitching to investors.

In a startup, the technical co-founder plays a pivotal role, which is the role I took on while working with my partners. After initial negotiations about the product, I gained a clearer understanding of what the prototype needed to achieve, the role of various technologies mentioned in the job posting, and an initial idea of how to build the product. From the moment I read about and applied for the position, I believed I could successfully blend these technologies to create a functional product. It was a creative mindset, driven by my confidence that I could turn my product vision into reality.

Shortly after starting work on the project, with the assistance of a remote student, we built the first prototype. Our confidence was so high in its quality and functionality that we connected it to the designated hardware without thorough testing. It was only months later, when I had access to the physical hardware and performed the first tests, that our confidence was validated: the software communicated successfully with the hardware. This marked a significant milestone, confirming the proof of concept.

However, the product was still far from completion; it was merely a technological demonstration that we could showcase to external stakeholders for feedback and improvement ideas. The role of piecing the system together aligned perfectly with my job description. I tinkered with various technologies to make the product work. The fact that it succeeded on the first test was a testament to the "if you can imagine it, you can build it" theory. It bolstered my confidence in tackling any challenge. The product was essentially assembled from different software components and tailored to our needs. While security was a concern from the start, other software aspects like quality, reliability, and scalability were not within the scope at this stage. At the time, it seemed like the right approach: code the feature, test it on the hardware, and gather feedback from potential users. High speed, frequent changes, and small victories were part of my daily routine.

This hacking and tinkering phase continued for a while, and I managed all aspects of the code and application deployment single-handedly. This initial prototype became our basis when we approached a corporate accelerator, and it marked our first concrete achievement as a company.

The technologies we used were diverse, and the technological roadmap was still undefined due to evolving requirements. As we entered the acceleration phase, we engaged with more influential prospects who had a deeper understanding of the expectations for our software tool. Each discussion and presentation revealed new aspects of the picture. We learned about crucial missing features our software lacked. Alongside a working student, I remained active in software development and expanded the technology stack to accommodate new features. I took on the role of a junior architect during this phase, marking my transformation from a hacker to an architect.

The transition from hacking to creating simpler architectures felt natural. With a better understanding of product requirements and customer expectations, defining the necessary technology stack to meet those needs became straightforward. Everything began to align, and technical decisions naturally stemmed from business requirements. Our focus shifted to delivering the product to early customers, allowing them to use the software for its original purpose, even if it deviated slightly from the ideal "bug-free" path without encountering major issues.

In our initial prototype, we laid the groundwork for our software. Since then, we've made significant improvements to create a more user-friendly web interface, making it accessible to those less familiar with technical jargon. This shift has transformed our tool into something that's actually usable. During this phase, we've gained a clearer vision of what our software should look like as a marketable product.

We've identified the scope of our work, taken note of any limitations, outlined the technology requirements, and set expectations for deliverables. While the software continued to evolve, the pace of change slowed down. Our focus shifted towards adding new features that would enhance its value. At this stage, I remained the sole contributor, responsible for both coding and deployment.

Despite these ongoing developments, our software offered a reliable basic functionality. We've also thoroughly addressed specific scenarios and corner cases to demonstrate its capabilities more effectively. This second iteration served as a valuable tool for showcasing our product to potential financial investors.

Our company primarily operated in the business-to-business market, selling our product to other industrial companies. This meant that we needed a dependable, commercially mature product with scalability to ensure high customer satisfaction. Building such a comprehensive product required a significant investment of time and resources before we could start invoicing customers. We had to spend money upfront before generating any revenue.

As we initiated our first round of fundraising, my role as CTO evolved again. In addition to coding, I took on the responsibility of presenting our technical capabilities to potential investors and devising the future strategy for our technical team. We communicated our progress and expressed our desire to expand and strengthen our team for the development of a fully functional product. This transformation, from a junior architect to a part-time project manager, felt relatively smooth. My prior project management experience in a student organization likely contributed to this adaptability. Our budget and team size remained relatively modest, allowing me to draw from my previous experiences effectively.

Creating a technical product roadmap was challenging, as business requirements were still evolving. Nevertheless, I formulated a strategy to guide our future growth. My vision for the company at this stage involved hiring a select group of senior employees to oversee software architecture, development, and operations. I saw my role as providing support and guidance to these hires, helping them acclimate to the specifics of our industry. Over time, these senior employees would, in turn, train new recruits. They would serve as the masterminds of our software engineering efforts, collectively identifying skill gaps within the team and devising plans to address them. The goal was to create a self-sustaining system where newer hires gradually assumed coding responsibilities, allowing me to focus on emerging duties. This system was designed to scale until the project had all the necessary resources to become fully self-sustainable.

This strategy was presented to investors and accepted for execution after the fundraising round concluded. Shortly after, I began working on the plan and recruited experienced engineers to build the product. As many may know, finding high-quality software engineers can be challenging, and it often takes time to find the right fit. Fortunately, we found the right team fairly quickly, and by August 1, 2016, we were ready to begin. Our team consisted of a student engineer who had been with us from the early days, a senior backend engineer, and a freelance developer focusing on the front-end development of the application. We started in a room provided by the university incubator with a blank slate and a set of general requirements.

During that day, we dedicated our time to understanding the non-negotiable requirements of the application, its scope, and expected outcomes. We aimed to define a technology stack that was reliable, scalable, and aligned with the preferences of our potential customers.

This marked the beginning of the third and final major overhaul of our product's technology stack. The first prototype was hastily put together to prove the concept, and the second iteration was an incremental improvement over the initial proof-of-concept, with significant added functionality. Now, with the hiring of a senior software engineer and a better understanding of customer needs and expectations, I was ready to embark on the third rewrite of the product. In this new role, I saw it as my responsibility to transfer the knowledge I had gathered and provide our developers with the tools, support, and information they needed to excel in their tasks. My role was shifting once again, as I now worked at the intersection of customers' needs, business requirements, and the technical team.

Transitioning from pure engineering to taking on responsibility for a team and budget is a significant change that not everyone is willing to embrace. The required skill set evolves from solely focusing on one's technical work, which involves technical know-how, diligence, and a commitment to writing clean, readable code, to encompassing strong communication skills, negotiation, patience, understanding, and delegation. This shift represents a completely different set of skills that not every engineer is naturally inclined to master. Pursuing a career as an exceptional engineer with deep technical knowledge is a perfectly valid choice, and no one should be criticized for opting not to take on additional responsibilities that demand more soft skills. The obvious difference between the two skill sets highlights the significant changes in the CTO's role as a company grows.

The discrepancy in the roles a CTO must undertake as a company expands can create tension among the founding members. There are two potential paths to follow: one where the business side expects the CTO to remain deeply involved in development indefinitely, and the other where the CTO assumes a more managerial role, with less time spent on low-level code details. Neither choice is inherently better, and each is highly dependent on individual preferences. For me, the challenge of working at the intersection of business and technology was the more interesting path, offering greater potential for personal growth. I made the decision to pursue this path, develop my soft skills, learn to delegate, and trust the team to do their job effectively. While this decision aligned with the strategy set during the fundraising with investors, it also created tension with my co-founders because I spent less time coding.

The external tension with my co-founders regarding my

coding efforts also led to an internal conflict within me. I'm inherently a hacker, and I thrive on tackling challenging tasks and turning them from nothing (0) into something (1), as Peter Thiel aptly explained. This transformation process truly fascinates me, and I could spend endless hours tinkering with complex problems that others might consider unworthy or impossible. However, I acknowledge that I lack the formal training to turn these proof-of-concepts into large, scalable, and highly reliable products with efficient architectures. I made a conscious decision to trust experts in handling scalability issues, as I believed it was the right path for the product, the company, and myself.

Delegation is one of the first skills one must acquire, but it's not always evident to all founders. It can be in conflict with the desire for full control and the passion for handling every aspect of a startup. After delegation, clear and transparent communication is crucial to master. Communication is a complex skill that plays a vital role in avoiding and resolving conflicts. I found these soft skills incredibly intriguing. Understanding how people react to your actions and words is the opposite of coding, where everything is deterministic and under one person's control. While an "if (true)" statement will always produce the same result, the same spoken statement can be perceived very differently by different individuals.

Furthermore, these skills become even more critical as the company's product portfolio expands. Most companies start with a single product, which may either succeed immediately or require several iterations to achieve success. As the CTO, my responsibility is to adapt the technology stack to the specific needs of the business case we are addressing. My focus should be on meeting our business targets. The initial product sets the foundation, and eventually, it becomes necessary to diversify the company's offerings. This could involve extending services to existing customers or developing entirely new, complementary products. In both scenarios, new technology stacks and team compositions will be required. At this point, I must be prepared to step back from the initial product, which I may have an emotional attachment to, and delegate authority to others. I must trust that these team members, under my guidance, will excel, perhaps even outperforming my own work. Without effective delegation and the ability to let go of emotional attachments, such a transition is unlikely to succeed.

Empowering team members and entrusting them with significant responsibilities is a way of nurturing a new generation of leaders within the company. This new generation of leaders is essential for the exponential growth and diversification of our startup. While this role as a creator of future leaders may not always be obvious or explicitly discussed, it is observed in many successful companies.

The changes in the role of a Chief Technology Officer (CTO) may not be immediately obvious or self-explanatory, especially for an early-stage developer. Like many challenges in a startup, there's often a steep learning curve involved, and that's what you're seeking. The role of a non-technical founder is not necessarily easier to master, but it might involve a somewhat different set of skills. For instance, a founder seeking investors in a seed round will still be involved in fundraising in later rounds, but with different strategies, advisors, and financial considerations.

The role of a CTO can vary depending on the nature of the startup:

- In a deep tech startup, where innovative technology is developed (possibly as a spin-off from a university or a garage project), the technical founder often has a strong connection to the technology and is the visionary behind its development. Here, the business evolves alongside the technology, such as in semiconductor manufacturing.

- In a company with an innovative business model, the products or services offered may have been in the market for a while. However, the founder has found a new, customer-friendly way to generate profit from existing technologies, with minimal technological innovation, as seen in low-cost airlines.

In the first scenario, the technical founder is deeply involved in the product's technological development, while in the second scenario, the focus is more on building the technology stack to support the innovative business model. The nature of the startup is generally known from day one, and the CTO should have a broad idea of what to expect. Sometimes, startups blend technical and business expertise, resulting in a hybrid where technology and business complement each other. This synergy can be beneficial, providing strong business opportunities and funding for further research. However, it can also be challenging if the business pushes immature technology to market or if technology doesn't align with the business strategy.

As the CTO's role changes with evolving tasks, it also impacts the founding team. The entire team needs to adapt to changing responsibilities. This adds a new dimension to the CTO's transformation. Unlike the evolution from a hacker to an architect and then to a manager, where roles within the team change, the founding team members tend to stay the same. Companies usually have the same core team working together, each with their strengths and unique qualities. While the team may expand with the hiring of new senior managers to meet the company's growing needs, the core team remains stable. Despite evolving requirements, individuals within the team tend to change slowly and infrequently. This applies to both you and your team members.

Recognizing this fact is essential because it will guide you throughout your journey with the team. Understanding the causes of conflicts within the team, the sources of satisfaction, and the areas of concern, as well as the aspects that work well, is crucial. It's important to note that your role isn't to change others, and I don't recommend attempting it as it can drain your energy with uncertain results. Instead, you should focus on setting boundaries for what you're willing to accept and when to provide feedback or accept facts as they are. This is a learning process, and initially, you might believe you can change aspects of your team that you dislike. While some small changes may succeed, most won't. Your best approach is to learn to leverage the strengths of your team members, empower them, and thrive on the diversity they bring. The results will be unexpected but with positive outcomes for both you and the team's efficiency.

The transformation into a role that involves leading people is significant and differs greatly from previous roles. It requires patience, effective communication skills, and self-reflection capabilities. Instead of looking to correct others, start by examining your own strengths and weaknesses. Not everyone is inclined to embrace this role and invest the time and effort required to master it. However, like any other skill, it can be developed with practice and dedication, depending solely on the individual - whether they're a CTO, CEO, CFO - and their willingness to grow in this direction. In this role, one must be open to receiving feedback and implementing it. It's a challenging change that happens slowly and necessitates profound personal growth. Maintaining a belief that this change is for the better, one must persist until satisfactory results are achieved.

How do you measure the results of this change? This is a subjective matter. From my experience, what works is increased employee satisfaction, improved productivity, and personal enthusiasm for working with the team. While it's impossible to satisfy every team member simultaneously, overall harmony and strong cohesion within the team can be observed. You'll learn to delegate, support, and trust your team members. It may seem like you're losing control as you empower team members and assign tasks to your colleagues, and in a way, you are. However, you have to trust that your team will work towards achieving the company's vision, even if they do things differently than you would. You must believe that the overall result is greater than what you could achieve alone. Once the process is fine-tuned, and the team is well-structured, it will function like an unstoppable living organism. It will present new, unexpected opportunities and allow your company to grow at a faster rate than you could achieve alone.

Once the CTO has successfully transitioned into a people management role, another upgrade awaits: taking on the responsibilities of representing the company externally. Public speaking and presentation skills, often associated with sales and communication managers, can be immensely beneficial to a CTO as well. In this role, you'll be required to deliver technical presentations at conferences and participate in panel discussions in front of large audiences. Like any other skill, presentation and public speaking can be improved with practice. You don't need to become the greatest orator in the world, but you should be able to confidently discuss topics related to your company's field of expertise.

One of the biggest challenges that engineer CTOs face is the perception that the time they spend on presentations takes away from critical technology development and is, in essence, wasted. There's some truth to this, as tasks that you used to handle on your own now need to be delegated. Code reviews and pull requests must be managed differently. It may feel like you're losing control, but this transition is essential for both your personal growth and the company's success.

The time you invest in representing your company externally isn't 100% efficient when viewed as an individual activity. However, it's crucial for your success because it helps promote your personal brand, your company, and its technology. Many discussions may seem unproductive, with partners who are more interested in their offerings than in what you have to offer. In such situations, consider shifting your perspective. Instead of thinking about how these people can help you, think about how you can help and be of service to them. You don't need to buy into everything others are selling, but you can provide references to partners who may urgently need certain services or offer non-monetary assistance that can benefit your counterparts.

Helping others triggers the release of oxytocin, serotonin, and dopamine in your brain, which can improve your mood and reduce stress. In essence, helping others is a way of helping yourself.

It's not up to you to judge how or if you've helped others. Having a positive attitude and taking action to assist should be part of your character. This extends to various situations, even in negotiations with your company's suppliers. Eventually, price negotiations will come into focus. As you negotiate for lower prices to protect your company's resources and set strict limits, you might find that you're pushing for a price well below what the salesperson initially offered, nearly wiping out their profit margin. The seller may perceive this as being taken advantage of or as an attempt to deceive them.

However, from a broader perspective, you've helped the seller achieve their expected margin for this particular deal. In a larger sense, you've brought them one step closer to their annual sales target by closing another customer. If you have a strong reputation in the industry, your patronage can bring additional advertising to the seller, offsetting the losses in this deal. It's crucial always to behave courteously and respectfully towards your counterparts, as this approach tends to yield more positive results than any other tactic.

The role of a Chief Technology Officer (CTO) in a fast-growing company is crucial, even though it often stays in the background while the CEO gets all the media attention for announcements like new investments, product releases, or office moves. This is a common expectation in society, and as a CTO, it's important to accept this reality.

While it might seem easy to work behind the scenes, especially if you come from an engineering background, you may still desire external recognition for your contributions. However, this recognition may come in a different form. It will be in the form of appreciation from your team, the respect you earn from your leadership, and the positive feedback you receive from the technical community.

Think of it like watching ducks on a lake. They appear content and peaceful on the surface, but beneath the water, they are paddling vigorously to reach their goals. Similarly, a CTO's role involves a lot of hard work and dedication that often goes unseen. You must always appear confident and in control, just like those calm ducks.

Despite working closely with a team, the CTO role can feel lonely at times. You might miss having a boss to talk to when things aren't going well, or colleagues for casual office chats. You have to maintain a facade of confidence even when facing tough decisions. You play a central role in the company, contributing significantly to its success, even if not everyone sees the hard work happening behind the scenes.

In essence, being a CTO is like being that duck gliding gracefully on the surface while working tirelessly beneath it to move forward.

Collecting high-hanging fruits in your work can be challenging. These fruits are difficult to reach, but the satisfaction of harvesting them makes the effort worthwhile. As a leader, whether you're in a CTO role or any other position with team responsibilities, it's crucial to give credit to your team for their achievements and to remain humble about your own contributions. Your acknowledgments must be genuine, as insincerity will be noticed by your team.

When you consistently give credit and acknowledgments, you may find that few people recognize your contributions to the company. This is because you're accountable for your actions and don't have a manager to report to regarding your targets. The company's board and general roadmap provide direction, but credit is rarely given when things go smoothly. It's easy to get caught up in always wanting more and forgetting to appreciate your past successes. Success can blind you to why you started these endeavors in the first place.

Conversely, when things go wrong and targets aren't met, especially on the technical side, you'll often be the first to take responsibility for the failure. As the CTO, you're expected to ensure that things run smoothly for the company's benefit. This imbalance between receiving praise for success and being blamed for failure places a significant psychological burden on you.

All the patents, innovations, and processes you've established that work flawlessly are often taken for granted until the moment they fail. When a process breaks down, fingers point at you, and everyone forgets about the things that are still working. Recognizing this fact is essential for maintaining your motivation and energy. You can achieve this by communicating with your team, addressing issues, or simply taking a break and treating yourself to something special.

A similar blame game occurs when your work as a CTO, or in any role within a startup or large organization, isn't adequately communicated and marketed. In the early days of a startup, your role is crucial to its success, as the technical foundation is being established. Decisions you make in these early stages can have a profound impact. Over time, your workload may decrease as technical processes become established, and your decisions become smaller in scale.

However, a common situation arises where a simple demonstration is needed, and you and your team create a prototype quickly, not considering all aspects of quality and scalability. As the project evolves, it turns into a full-fledged product, and you may wonder why you didn't build it more stably. Despite these concerns, it continues to work, but you're stuck with an old, unstable technology. This guilt stems from business pressure to deliver quickly, the need to keep costs low, and the belief that it's a short-lived product. This pattern might repeat with subsequent projects, but you'll gradually improve with each experience.

As the company's product portfolio expands, your responsibilities grow to encompass all the products the company is developing. You are expected to become an expert in everything the company is working on, but this can be quite challenging. Balancing the need to understand every function in the company with the demand to present the product portfolio to the board members can be demanding. Some may find satisfaction in the former tasks, while others may prefer the latter.

When the company's growth stabilizes, your workload and job type will change slightly. The CFO, CEO, and COO will become more involved, seeking explanations for your reduced involvement compared to the early days. They may wonder why you can afford to be more relaxed about decisions while they work tirelessly. It's easy to forget the effort you put in during the critical early days when your role was pivotal. Only a few will truly appreciate that your role has evolved with the company's needs.

There may be pressure to take on more tasks beyond your current responsibilities just to align with the rest of the management. This workload imbalance among managing partners can signal a dysfunctional team. Ideally, team members should work closely together, accepting each other's decisions based on their roles. However, this discrepancy is often more common in young startups. Founders should be aware of this to prevent disruptions in achieving the company's growth targets.

In a young startup, the role of the Chief Technology Officer (CTO) undergoes a transformation. The CTO evolves from an initial hacker into an architect, project manager, team lead, and eventually, a senior manager with external representation tasks. This rapid evolution requires a diverse skill set, and some people thrive on constant role changes, while others may find it challenging. It's crucial for expectations within the founding team to align. If a hacker wants to remain a hacker but co-founders expect them to become a project manager, problems can arise. The hacker-CTO may dislike the project manager role and struggle to perform, leading to frustration among co-founders who expected different results.

These situations can be resolved with understanding and acceptance from both sides. A hacker-CTO should be allowed to remain a hacker if that's their passion, and co-founders should provide the freedom to grow and acquire new skills, as long as it benefits the company. Every person's unique contributions should be appreciated, and they should be given space to pursue their own goals and paths. In an environment where trust, support, and understanding prevail, individuals can thrive. Embracing diversity, even when it's challenging, often leads to unexpected and beautiful projects.

In founding teams, achieving mutual understanding isn't always easy, and there can be a lack of respect for each other's decisions. This often happens because everyone has different expectations, leading to dissatisfaction on one or both sides. Unfortunately, it's common for the Chief Technology Officer (CTO) to succumb to pressure and resign from their role. I've observed that, despite their critical initial role, CTOs are frequently replaced as a company evolves. This outcome is regrettable for everyone involved, including the project itself, as finding and training a replacement can be challenging. The new CTO usually aligns more with the other managers' expectations, which might have been the case with the initial CTO when they joined the team. Departing CTOs often follow one of two paths: they either return to a pure engineering role, especially if they're passionate about coding, or they pursue another middle- or upper-management job in a different company to align with their career aspirations.

In my own experience as the technical co-founder, I started as a hands-on coder, which was a short-term role I played in the company. I made it clear from the beginning that my vision was to build a self-sufficient, growing team. My plan was to recruit senior talent as soon as possible to handle the development tasks. Perhaps because of my previous experiences, I naturally took on recruiting responsibilities and felt comfortable giving presentations about our technology to different audiences. I still enjoy the diversity of working with people, empowering them, and learning how to manage emotions effectively. I firmly believe that when you provide your team with the right resources and empower them, they can achieve results that surpass your wildest expectations. I ended up assuming this leadership role in the startup during our second or third year of operation. However, the management team didn't accept this shift, as they expected me to continue playing a software development role even in the fourth and fifth year of operation.

I no longer felt confident in getting my hands dirty with every line of code in the application. My "hacker" spirit could prototype concepts on a small scale, but I preferred handing them over to more experienced developers to ensure quality and scalability. I had clearly communicated this goal when we closed our financing round. Due to budget constraints and a desire to keep costs low, the team consisted mainly of working students and recent graduates. While they were highly skilled in their respective areas, they lacked guidance on code and architecture from a senior figure. This conflict between me as the technical founder and the business partners persisted throughout our journey. The business side saw attending conferences and going public as a waste of time, but I viewed it as an opportunity to raise awareness about the company and attract highly skilled individuals who could strengthen our team.

In this conflict, I chose to follow my own path, which led me away from coding. Was it the right decision? Was it wrong? It was right for me because I followed my dreams and pursued what I was passionate about. From feedback provided by former employees, they were comfortable working together, and from the company's perspective, having one more junior developer wouldn't have made a significant difference. However, it was wrong to let this conflict persist. I eventually accepted that my business partners would never understand or support my career decision. Coming to terms with this realization brought me much-needed relief and self-satisfaction. I still believe I acted in the best interest of the company, even without their approval. I saw my role as building a team and enabling new leaders to emerge. I trusted and empowered them while providing the necessary support to excel in their roles. When you have the right team, they will take care of the company's products, leading to greater customer satisfaction, which is crucial for successful, exponential growth.

5.

ENJOYING THE JOURNEY THROUGH UNCERTAINTY

When I embarked on my journey as an entrepreneur, I was filled with excitement and anticipation. I looked forward to tackling the diverse and complex tasks that come with starting a new venture. The prospect of meaningful work, quick decision-making, and the potential for exponential growth drew me into this unknown territory. I had already taken several entrepreneurship courses during my time at university, absorbing the vocabulary commonly used by founders. I read books filled with accounts of successful entrepreneurs and eagerly listened to founder presentations. Often, these founders would describe the journey as challenging, full of unknowns, yet incredibly rewarding and worthwhile. It was a captivating narrative.

Most of the stories I encountered, whether heard or read, were success stories. They recounted major contract signings, successful fundraising rounds, and key hires. While people did acknowledge that for every success story, there were many failed attempts and missed opportunities, as determined and confident founders, we tended to focus on the successes and downplay the failures. We convinced ourselves that we could overcome any obstacles that came our way. However, this "somehow" wasn't something we could learn in school or find in books on how to navigate such situations.

Our society tends to celebrate and highlight winners, a trend that extends to the startup ecosystem. Every city, every incubator boasts about its success stories, holding them up as examples. These are the startups that have achieved remarkable success, and their achievements are proudly showcased by their supporting partners, such as incubators, accelerators, and universities. These partners want to demonstrate their expertise and knowledge, so they emphasize their success stories. When was the last time you heard someone pitch their journey of failure over five years and returning to a corporate job? It's a cycle where a select few are continually praised for their successes, while the rest are forgotten in the shadows of obscurity.

In the midst of this cycle of celebrating extraordinary successes, many enterprises that have achieved significant success in terms of business growth and profitability are overlooked. Then there are those whose business cases don't meet expectations, leading them to close their operations for various reasons. For the former group—the successful but lesser-known ones—the term "hidden champion" is often used, and it's an apt description. Yet, it remains a mystery why we hear so little about these companies that have clearly done many things right. One common thread among all startup companies, though rarely publicized, is the emotional rollercoaster they ride. These emotional ups and downs are a constant part of an entrepreneur's life, but they are often omitted from the glamorous success stories that only highlight the highs. Presenting failures is considered a sign of weakness and goes against the prevailing spirit of the ecosystem, which prefers to focus on the positive.

In a startup environment, the founding team operates in a highly uncertain world. While the business plan outlines assumptions and expectations about the company's future, it's often based on statistics and theoretical reports rather than the real-world dynamics of the economy. While it provides guidance, founders must always be vigilant for new opportunities and seize them as they arise. There's no guaranteed formula for success in this ever-changing landscape, though some indicators may point in the right direction.

This volatile environment, coupled with the desire to be the first to identify and seize opportunities, can be emotionally taxing for founders. It's essential to acknowledge these challenges and work with them, rather than trying to suppress them. Suppressing such thoughts and feelings can lead to more stress, whereas being aware of them and listening to them is a healthier approach.

In our daily lives, we encounter situations where some actions go as planned while others end up being less successful. Even simple tasks like cooking a meal can yield either a delicious dish or an unfortunate outcome that we quickly forget about. As humans, we've learned to handle these small successes and failures without much difficulty. However, for entrepreneurs, these experiences can be more intense due to the high stakes involved.

I recall a series of events early in my startup journey that taught me a valuable lesson. We were awaiting the evaluation of our grant application, which we believed had a high chance of success. Simultaneously, we were waiting to hear back about our application to join a corporate accelerator program where our chances were slim. As fate would have it, our grant application was rejected, while we were accepted into the corporate accelerator. This experience taught us not to take anything for granted and to avoid considering anything as certain until it's either happened or contracts are signed.

In the world of startups, some actions lead to expected, positive outcomes, while others may result in failure. This is something everyone can understand and expect to encounter. While some may debate whether everything happens for a higher reason, that's a discussion for another time. What's remarkable about these actions is often their timing. I vividly remember when we received the rejection for the grant application on a casual early afternoon. The disappointment was palpable, and many questions arose: Why are we doing this? What did we do wrong? How can we improve? We needed time to digest the news and accept it. The surprise came just a few hours later when we learned of our acceptance into the accelerator program. Within a short span of time, we went from feeling demotivated to suddenly feeling optimistic and empowered.

Did we do anything differently? Not much, or at least nothing we were consciously aware of. It was the same team, working on the same project, following the same flow that we presented to both parties. However, each party evaluated the idea differently, leading to different outcomes. This left me feeling confused because I didn't know whether to be sad about missing out on the grant or happy about the accelerator opportunity. It felt like trying to cry with one eye while laughing with the other, which, if possible, I would have done. My emotions kept shifting rapidly in the immediate hours after receiving the news. One moment, I felt sad about the missed grant, then I remembered the accelerator and all the promising opportunities it offered, making me feel happy. But then, the memory of the missed grant would resurface, and I started questioning myself again. It was a never-ending cycle of emotions that persisted throughout the day. There are no words to adequately express the rollercoaster of emotions I experienced, oscillating between joy and sadness in such a short time. Handling such strong emotions within a brief period was something we couldn't have been prepared for.

Amidst this whirlwind of conflicting emotions, I found myself retreating into my inner thoughts, pondering various "why" scenarios and trying to make sense of "what" had happened, what was "right," and what was "wrong." It was a self-imposed internal turmoil, almost like punishing myself for what I perceived as a failure, as if there had to be a penalty for not meeting the expected standards of success. For a short while, until news from the accelerator arrived, I immersed myself in building various imaginary scenarios for the future, heavily influenced by my momentary emotions.

As time passed, the intense emotions began to fade, allowing us to analyze the situation more rationally. It was akin to seeing the glass as both half-empty and half-full at the same time. We acknowledged the feedback we received from the grant reviewers and started planning a second submission, for which we were still eligible. Simultaneously, we recognized the significant opportunity offered by the corporate accelerator and began preparing for the acceleration period. These two actions were emotionally charged for me, providing a rollercoaster ride of emotions, much like what I had experienced earlier. This left a profound impression on me, to the extent that in the future, I would often act with detachment, sometimes seeming distant, and always striving to be rational when faced with events labeled as having a strong impact on our business. With very few exceptions, I would accept things as they came, without doubting or questioning my abilities. This situation highlighted how I had attached "good" and "bad" labels to events, which were highly subjective and based on my expectations of how things should unfold, as well as the expectations imposed on me by others. These labels were reference points to external narratives and standards that I had unquestioningly accepted.

The result of this labeling was evident in my emotional reactions when independent evaluators applied opposite labels to the same actions. It served as a powerful lesson that the labels I subjectively attach can significantly influence my perceived reality. I would then proceed to run various scenarios in my mind about how the future might unfold, which, in turn, triggered more emotions. This, too, was a misconception, as all these potential outcomes existed solely in my imagination and held no power over external reality. Amidst the elaborate mental spectacles I created, the world continued to operate as usual. The labels only impacted my perception, while the external reality remained unchanged, following its normal course. This underscored the importance of self-control in refraining from attaching labels dictated by external standards, especially those I might not even believe in, and accepting events in their simple, unadorned nature. To do so without internal suffering requires unwavering focus on the ultimate goal, resisting distractions and temptations, and taking steps that bring us closer to our vision.

In this context, it's important not to get caught up in labeling events and living solely for their outcomes, which may conform to external standards. The key lesson here is to cherish the journey itself. Embrace the opportunity to apply for the grant, appreciate the feedback received, and recognize the dedication required to prepare the bureaucratic documents that convey our ideas. As it's often said, it's about the journey, not just the end goal. This was one of the early lessons in a series of events that emphasized the value of savoring the moment as it unfolds.

We initially felt disappointed when our grant application was rejected, but a few hours later, we were overjoyed when an unexpected success came our way. If an outsider were observing us, they would likely view such an opportunity as a great blessing: the freedom and courage to apply for a grant, the effort put into crafting a business plan, and the presentation in front of a large corporation. They would admire our determination and perhaps even envy the fact that we pursued these stages. To me, it seemed like something anyone could do if they truly desired it. I had overlooked this perspective because of my preconceived notions.

To align with entrepreneurial norms, we later focused on highlighting our successes. We prominently displayed the accelerator's logo on our slide deck, mentioned them in every investor and customer meeting, and took pride in our achievements. The failure of our grant application, which had seemed like an obvious outcome to many, was soon forgotten and rarely discussed. These actions were primarily aimed at saving face and projecting confidence, driven by the labels imposed by common standards. We communicated only the perceived positive outcomes to demonstrate our strength and control over our work. In doing so, we perpetuated a cycle of promoting success while downplaying rejections, constructing our own idealized reality.

This series of events marked the initial step in learning to embrace the journey as it unfolds. I realized that I'm too limited to fully understand everything within the broader perspective. I needed to work with the resources I had to create a positive physical reality with a focus on the end result. Initially, I stopped dwelling on the 'why' because 'why' is a question tied to the past. It's concerned with yesterday and the days before, things we can no longer change. It's a waste of time, energy, and valuable mental resources to dwell on the past, something beyond our control. Not only does dwelling on the past under these circumstances hold us back, but it also robs us of a more crucial resource: the present moment.

During my introspective moments, I contemplated various scenarios rooted in my current emotions, projecting them onto an imagined future. This provided some relief in handling inner conflicts, but it was also a futile expenditure of time and energy because it fixated on an element outside our control: the future

The solution that has proven effective is to focus solely on the present day, as it's the only time we can control. This approach allows me to relax and enjoy events as they come, giving me a sense of power over my actions in the here and now. While I still keep a clear vision of the impact I want to achieve with my startup, my primary focus is on tackling the immediate tasks at hand.

I no longer dwell on why others have succeeded while we faced challenges. I've learned to disregard the long-term effects of individual evaluations because they are too distant to impact us significantly. Instead, I've embraced living in the moment and taking action in the present. This has been one of the most valuable lessons in my entrepreneurial journey because I couldn't foresee the future challenges or their magnitude. I've learned to handle unexpected situations with mindfulness, addressing them as they arise without retreating into a world of fantasy.

I've found serenity in accepting that issues, troubles, challenges, and unforeseen events are part and parcel of this journey. Rather than allowing them to distract or demotivate me, I acknowledge their presence and deal with them promptly. Ignoring them only increases the workload. What I've learned is that every problem has a solution. So, my approach is to acknowledge their presence, assign the necessary priority, and always bear in mind that there's a solution. I actively choose to believe that there's a solution because that's how problems ultimately get resolved. Once I've acknowledged this fact, these issues and troubles become tasks, just like any other in my backlog.

To organize these tasks, I employ the Eisenhower Matrix, which categorizes events by urgency and importance:

- Urgent and Important: Requires immediate action.
- Not Urgent but Important: Prioritized and handled when time permits.
- Urgent but Not Important: Delegated to others if possible.
- Not Urgent and Not Important: Low priority; may not need attention.

Before reacting emotionally to a problem and imagining its outcome, I remind myself that problems always have solutions. It may not be immediately obvious or may take time to find the right solution, but there's always one to be found. With time and experience, as your company matures and you understand your customers and niche better, you'll notice that many problems are recurring. You can then apply previously identified solutions and make them disappear.

Even seemingly significant problems can be broken down into smaller ones until you identify the root cause. The solution will reveal itself, reinforcing the belief that every problem has a solution.

One common source of energy drain is a multitude of small tasks that need attention. These small tasks often take only 5-10 minutes to complete but can be mentally taxing to start. We've all been in situations where we complain about the tasks at hand. In reality, once you begin these small, dreaded tasks, you've already completed half the work. By developing a habit of finishing these tasks as they arrive, I've found relief in promptly closing these topics. This approach works well for me, even with interruptions from other tasks. It's easier to send a quick email reply than to postpone it and add it to a to-do list for later.

One common perception about startup founders, as well as ambitious managers and consultants, is that they work long hours and are always busy. This holds true, especially when someone is running their own business, where they often find themselves juggling numerous tasks, even the smaller ones. During the early stages of a company, when many processes need to be set up, this busy lifestyle is indeed the norm. However, it's just as crucial to prioritize taking breaks.

Back when I worked in consulting, there were days when I put in very long hours. I understood that, to a certain extent, these extra hours were accumulating and could be compensated for when the opportunity arose. Typically, there was one day a week dedicated to administrative tasks, which was a lighter workload day. Overall, you had a manager and an IT system that, in a broad sense, kept track of your working hours. However, when I started my own startup, it was only me who could decide when to put in extra hours and when to rest.

Recognizing when to step away from work, to say, "I'm done for today," was the challenging part and required training. You understand the importance of your company, that others are relying on you, yet you must still make that call to take a break. Of course, you must also be able to differentiate between important and less important tasks. Overworking yourself is akin to working in short bursts, and if you want to achieve long-term success, finding the much-needed rest is crucial.

As a founder, it's easy to fall into the trap of overworking due to the open tasks and societal expectations placed on this role. I strongly believe that the emphasis on rest and recovery is not given enough attention. Some have recognized this, and those who have tend to fare better. It's important to establish clear boundaries between work and your personal life and to respect those boundaries.

The work of a founder is intellectual work, and its output cannot be easily quantified by the number of hours worked. In fact, putting in long hours might even be counterproductive for decision-making because exhaustion can lead to different decisions compared to when you have a clear mind. Respecting the boundaries you've set for yourself can help maintain a clear mind to thoroughly analyze all the factors involved in a decision.

Each person reacts differently, and it's essential to know yourself well to make the most of your capabilities. For instance, I am an early bird, and I've discovered that I make significant decisions in the morning. Afternoons and evenings are reserved for creative work and repetitive tasks. Through trial and error, I've also learned that depriving myself of sleep for extended periods changes my decision-making process. In this state, I feel more capable and confident in making short-term decisions, such as choosing between blue or green colors. However, it becomes more challenging to make strategic decisions.

I arrived at these insights through experience, deliberately or unintentionally exposing myself to various situations. Such experiences come with time as you grow with your startup. In the initial months of the company, many small tasks will demand your attention. However, as time goes by and your team grows, the nature of your responsibilities will change. You'll come to understand the importance of rest and allocate time for it. The sooner you start taking care of yourself, both mentally and physically, the better it is in the long run for you and your project.

When talking to various people, I've noticed a common impression about founders – they often seem incredibly busy. It's almost as if they believe that being constantly busy is a measure of their success and worth. Some choose to brand themselves as always swamped, frequently pushing meetings and replies due to their packed schedules.

Postponing requests due to a busy calendar can be a legitimate action, but it loses its legitimacy when this behavior continues over a long time, when the reasons for delay seem trivial, and when there are no tangible results to show for all the overwork. For instance, consider a declined meeting request for a Monday morning, with the request to reschedule to the afternoon due to an urgent task. This seems reasonable initially. However, it becomes questionable when this "urgent" task has been known for two weeks and hasn't been addressed promptly. Moreover, the rescheduled meeting never happens, and there are no updates for a week.

When such occurrences happen occasionally, they are understandable, but when they become a pattern, it raises concerns about the priorities and work ethics of the other party. While explanations for being busy might make sense, they often don't reasonably justify significant delays. This behavior implies that the other party has chosen to label themselves as "overly busy," and this can be seen as a decision not to be judged. However, it also conveys a message that your matter is less important than everything else they're doing, which can be counterproductive within a team and demotivating.

The reasons behind such behavior can vary, and each case has its unique aspects. One observation relates to cultural differences. Coming from a German working culture, I noticed a difference when working with French colleagues. It became apparent that the French tend to start work later than the Germans; almost everyone begins later. What puzzled me initially was the significant number of requests that came in on Friday afternoons, starting around 4 PM. It was precisely when the Germans were gearing up for the weekend that the French became hyperactive. Strangely, it was only on Fridays, and it was always in the afternoon, just before the weekend.

Initially, I was frustrated. There was ample time during the other four working days, even on Friday, so why did everything suddenly become urgent when most people were about to start their weekend? This pattern continued with different individuals, and there didn't seem to be a reasonable explanation. It appeared to me that work was mainly getting done on Friday afternoons with my French colleagues.

Instead of resisting this trend, which I couldn't change anyway, I decided to accept it. I realized that Friday mornings were ideal for tasks that required my full attention since nobody would bother with requests during that time. Then, around 4 PM, the flood of questions and requests began like clockwork. I answered them with a smile on my face, enjoying the peace and quiet in the office as everyone else had left for the weekend. Interestingly, most of these requests were small things – modifying access permissions, notifying about document updates, vacation requests, or quick updates on customer progress. They could be handled in 5-10 minutes. I learned to appreciate their presence, either by addressing them or ignoring them, and then I'd start the week by tackling any open items from Friday evening.

The hidden message I received through these small requests on Friday afternoons seemed to say, "Hey, we work hard, even on Friday evenings, we don't go home early." While everyone has the freedom to organize their work as they see fit, what I find problematic is when this is used to compare and judge others, implying, "I'm still working on Friday evenings; what are you doing?"

While navigating the uncertain world of a startup, I've discovered the joy of working with people from diverse cultures and backgrounds. What I've learned is that everyone has good intentions, desires acceptance within the community, and wants to contribute their insights. I've also come to understand that each individual is unique and deserves personalized attention and appreciation. As a result, I don't place too much emphasis on working hours or the time of day when effort is invested. In the software engineering industry, flexibility in this regard is possible. I've made it clear to my team that what matters most to me are the results. I'm willing to provide support and assistance as needed, without being concerned if an engineer works during the day or night, or if their schedule varies from day to day, as long as we achieve the results we've agreed upon. I've learned to thrive in this environment of uncertainty by believing in the power of the team and placing trust in its members. Therefore, I'm not impressed by requests that come in late at night or on a Friday afternoon.

However, not everyone on the team shared this perspective and insisted on a fixed work schedule. When strict rules were imposed, I noticed an immediate decrease in the team's motivation and efficiency. While everyone adhered to their prescribed work hours, the enthusiasm for the work waned, and project deadlines were consistently missed. People no longer felt empowered; they were simply following one set of rules for everyone. I observed that code commits that used to occur on a rainy weekend or during a vacation day when someone had some free time ceased to happen, even though everyone was fulfilling their contractual work hours. This lack of trust in the team and the desire for control had unintended consequences on our product deliverables. The team's diversity and respect for individual preferences were overshadowed by a common standard that fell short of the team's potential. This serves as a clear example of how embracing diversity and leveraging it can directly impact product development.

In a similar vein, the entrepreneurial journey often involves envisioning both best and worst-case scenarios. Positive outcomes bring excitement, hope, and visions of a bright future. However, there's little time for rest because reaching one goal merely marks the start of the next. Positive scenarios fill us with enthusiasm and imagination. On the flip side, worst-case scenarios drain our energy and distract us from essential tasks. I've found that there is a lack of training and ready-made solutions for managing the emotions triggered by worst-case scenarios. As I mentioned earlier, problems and worst-case scenarios are inevitable parts of our journey, but there is always a solution to be found.

A highly effective approach when dealing with worst-case scenarios begins with acknowledging that these dire circumstances can and do occur. It's essential to consciously accept that the worst-case scenario is a reality that we must confront. Hiding from it or pretending it won't happen won't help. Embrace it as part of your journey.

As I move into the second stage of accepting the worst-case scenario, I find a sense of relief. The pressure seems to dissipate once I fully acknowledge this reality. At this point, I no longer dwell on questions like "Why me?" or "Why now?" It is what it is, and I must work with the situation at hand. Once I reach this stage, I can proceed to the final resolution stage: living in the present and taking action to improve the envisioned worst outcome.

During this stage, after acknowledging the presence of the worst-case scenario, I have the resources needed to take gradual steps to improve the situation. I've observed that, with a structured approach, the worst-case scenario can always be enhanced, even if only slightly.

The extent of improvement is a personal matter, often requiring significant preparation and dedication. This can involve extensive research, education, or previous practical experience. It requires an active effort to make a positive change. This process applies to significant events, such as the survival of a company, as well as smaller events like the fear of presenting in front of a large audience.

For instance, fear of presenting often stems from imagining various failures, like technical glitches or forgetting your speech. Once you acknowledge and accept these fears as part of reality, you can begin working to improve the worst-case scenario. For technical issues, you can ensure a thorough technical run-through before the presentation. To combat the fear of forgetting your speech, practice it until you know it by heart. Recognize that you're the expert in the room. As for the fear of public speaking, there are numerous strategies to help you overcome it.

Consider the example of presenting to different audiences—whether it's the general public, students, customers, or investors. Regardless of the circumstances, your level of preparation will ultimately determine your success. Preparation is a controllable factor that you can consistently improve upon.

Each individual can identify tools and strategies that work best for them during the preparation process. In my case, keeping a journal proved to be effective. I didn't write regularly, but I returned to it when my thoughts were in turmoil. Writing helped me organize my thoughts, starting with the initial situation, the events affecting it, and the potential outcome if no action was taken. Transferring ideas onto paper separated the noise from the concerns causing my worries. Once I pinpointed these primary sources of anxiety, I could move on to the next stage - preparing to improve the worst-case scenario and focusing my energy on constructive, solution-oriented thinking.

6.
RECOVERY IN HIGH PERFORMING ENVIRONMENTS

Starting a new journey, whether it's a vacation, a road trip, a new job, or a new company, is always filled with excitement and high expectations. This positive energy, combined with the hopes for success, fuels our determination to make things happen. However, at the beginning, we often find ourselves swamped with a variety of tasks, which can be overwhelming. Every action, email, phone call, trip, and conversation demands energy, both physically and mentally.

Operating in an environment of great uncertainty requires significant mental effort. Without the guarantee of success or a regular paycheck, our thoughts can wander into unknown territories. To keep these thoughts in check, it's crucial to ensure we get enough quality rest.

Unfortunately, rest is often overlooked in the early stages of a venture because of our strong drive to achieve our goals. We get caught up in a cycle of doing one more thing each day, thinking that completing small tasks will bring us closer to our objectives. The trap here is that our to-do list doesn't shrink; instead, it keeps growing as more tasks pile up.

Soon, exhaustion and demotivation set in because we've sacrificed sleep to tackle an ever-expanding list. This behavior mostly applies to operational tasks and less to strategic decisions, which are harder to measure in terms of their impact on fatigue. Yet, these strategic decisions are crucial for long-term personal and entrepreneurial success and should be approached with careful consideration. In these cases, rest becomes vital to clear our minds of noise and focus on the strategic implications.

First and foremost, we must prioritize getting enough quality sleep. Sleep often seems like the first thing we can sacrifice for work, family, or personal time. There are plenty of resources available on the benefits of sleep and various strategies for optimizing it. I view sleep as a resource that requires effective management and should be treated with urgency and importance.

Personally, I am fortunate to be a healthy sleeper and make good use of this resource for recovery. Over time, I've learned my optimal sleep parameters, adjusting my schedule based on the tasks at hand, whether they excite me or bore me. For exciting, motivating tasks, I can manage with consistent five to six hours of sleep per night for a few weeks. Conversely, for tedious, repetitive tasks lacking excitement, I still feel tired even after getting eight to ten hours of sleep. I've noticed that less than five hours of sound sleep doesn't benefit my productivity or work quality in the long run.

The message here is simple: recognize sleep as a valuable resource and treat it as an asset. Ensure you get enough quality sleep, find what works best for you, and apply the methods that suit you. You can educate yourself about sleep using the many resources available and experiment with different approaches. The one thing you should not do is ignore the importance of sleep.

Next to sleep, there are friends and family who are often taken for granted, and their contribution to one's recovery and well-being is easily overlooked. Spending time with your best friends, openly discussing your project's progress and the challenges you're facing, is something that comes naturally. You listen to their stories as well, being a good and considerate friend, unconditionally. However, it's essential to notice that these conversations primarily revolve around you and your progress. You get a valuable opportunity to voice your concerns, successes, and plans. You may not always receive direct solutions but instead more questions about your concerns. Simply expressing your worries and ideas out loud to a willing listener is incredibly beneficial. It helps organize your thoughts and create a coherent narrative. Often, the solution emerges miraculously when you articulate your thoughts. The questions you receive shed new light on the topic, offering different perspectives. This process filters out the noise, and the imagined fears diminish when they are expressed in words in the real world. We expect similar behavior from mentors or coaches we explicitly hire for this purpose.

On the other hand, family and friends are taken for granted because they've been there since our earliest memories. We assume they'll always be there for us. We might feel bothered when our family calls us at inconvenient times or keep postponing our call back. This reading aims to help you recognize, be grateful for their presence, and acknowledge their significant contribution to your development. Everyone's circle of family and friends is unique, and some may have more favorable circumstances than others, but there's hardly anyone in this world who doesn't have at least one friend.

Use the time spent with family and friends as an opportunity to unwind from your daily struggles. Enjoy their presence and be mindful of their stories. Acknowledge and appreciate their contributions to your personal development, success, and well-being.

In the professional world, there are various roles at all levels that operate under high-stress and uncertain conditions. Every individual must recognize the importance of recovery and dedicate the necessary attention to it. The first step in solving a problem is recognizing and accepting it, and the solution will follow. These diverse sources of emotions and stress are more noticeable in small enterprises than in larger ones. Employees in larger corporations also face the issue of overwork due to a strong desire to impress and exceed targets. Decades ago, people got ulcers, whereas today, we experience burnouts. The nature of these stressors differs slightly between large corporations and young enterprises. In the latter, roles are rarely as clearly defined, and individuals often have to cover multiple roles that require different skill sets. To prevent the team from overworking, it's beneficial to establish structures and departments as soon as possible.

Similarly, in large corporations, departments and clear hierarchies effectively alleviate the pressure on individual employees. When startups collaborate with large corporations, they often find the long decision-making cycles and numerous stakeholders frustrating. These processes distribute the responsibility for a decision across multiple peers. For instance, a personal matter may initially be handled by a manager, then the HR department, and perhaps multiple HR employees, before escalating to a higher management level. By the time a decision reaches the top, much of the pressure has dissipated, and the information has been filtered to only the essentials. The input of a single individual becomes diluted within the mass, reducing the psychological pressure of making a single decision. In contrast, a startup founder may need to decide on personal matters for employees even up to a significant company size. After dealing with such cases, finding comfort and peace to return to one's family and get a good night's sleep isn't always easy.

People often endure a great deal, and it's remarkable how much a person can handle. Many prioritize work and achieving a sense of accomplishment over self-care and well-being. This can be likened to a bear emerging from hibernation with little fat and minimal resources to survive, desperately seeking food to avoid starvation. While humans don't have the same hibernation behavior as bears, they often push themselves to the limit, depleting their physical and mental resources, living day to day without considering the long-term consequences.

This situation can persist for years, as long as everything remains stable. But when change finally arrives, there are no reserves left, no plan in place, and a sense of futility sets in. One begins to question why they sacrificed so much and neglected important aspects of life.

I found myself in this situation after about five years on my journey. I was living on the edge, with a salary that barely covered basic necessities. I was even earning less than supermarket cashiers. I had maximized my network, made no personal investments, and denied myself any luxuries or pleasures. Strangely, I wasn't demotivated; in fact, I was committed to giving my all for the success of the company. I had settled into a complacent existence, content with a meager standard of living, and lacked the confidence to dream bigger or explore other possibilities. I unknowingly put immense pressure on my closest family and friends, emotionally burdening them, which I now see as a significant mistake.

In this state of low confidence and energy, I remained stagnant until a change in my environment occurred. Suddenly, I had exhausted all my resources to the point where I couldn't even afford quality rest and recovery. It was a wake-up call, reminding me that it's wrong to live with such low self-esteem and boundaries close to self-humiliation. I learned to appreciate even the smallest moments and simple things that contribute to my recovery.

I began to appreciate spending time with my loved ones and found solace in sports. I suddenly realized how much I enjoyed riding my mountain bike and how long it had been since I last took it out for a spin in nature. I also rediscovered my love for long swims in a nearby lake and the thrill of going on adventures in the nearby mountains. It wasn't that I hadn't done these activities before; it was just that I hadn't been fully engaged and satisfied while doing them.

Swimming in the lake and spending time there became my best way to recover after experiencing strong emotions. When I was there, I could set aside all my worries and be fully present. I could soak in the beautiful scenery, enjoy the company of people around me, and marvel at the adorable dogs. My fiancée and I discovered this place filled with positive energy, and we spent countless evenings and mornings on the pontoon by the lake. Whenever we had something big on our minds, we would head to the lake, embrace the silence, watch the graceful swans, and clear our thoughts. After returning from our lake retreat, we left our worries behind and approached problems with a fresh perspective.

This form of active recovery worked well for me. While swimming, biking, or running, my body was engaged in burning calories in a repetitive manner, allowing my mind to wander freely. Swimming, in particular, proved to be the most effective method for mental recovery. After about thirty minutes of continuous swimming, my body fell into a rhythm, and my mind had ample space to roam. No emails, no phone calls, and no interruptions in the middle of the lake. I recommend trying this experience, but if you choose swimming, always have a buoy with you for safety. You'll be amazed at the variety of thoughts that can pass through your mind in just one hour. It will change how you perceive time and help you understand the power of focused concentration in a short period. For me, this was an incredibly effective recovery method.

You may have noticed that all the sports I mentioned are individual activities. This was a deliberate choice because it gave me the freedom to train on my own schedule and terms. Training with a team would have required more coordination and social interaction, which I was already exhausted from in my work environment. If you have the resources and energy to overcome these challenges and embrace team sports—or better yet, prioritize them—it can be immensely rewarding. The benefits of teamwork far outweigh what an individual can achieve. However, I didn't have the energy for team sports at the time and chose to channel my maximum effort into individual exercises.

One notable advantage of individual sports is the complete control over your training schedule. You set your goals, create a plan, and execute it with discipline. The standards are your own, and it's your ambition that drives you to achieve those goals. This was important to me because I needed to prove to myself that I could set high standards and reach goals I never thought possible. I couldn't believe I could swim 3000 meters in a single lap, but with consistent training and patience, I achieved it. This boosted my confidence and self-trust, and it was essential for me to radiate that confidence and energy back to my startup team.

In your role as a founder, your well-being is closely tied to the success of your company. If you're in good health, your company is likely to thrive. Conversely, if your health suffers, it can negatively impact your business. This is a straightforward relationship that should be apparent in your professional career. Taking proactive steps to ensure your recovery is essential, and the method you choose depends on your individual preference.

The purpose of this chapter is to emphasize the importance of recovery. The examples I've shared are what I've found to work best for me, but they're not meant to serve as a manual for using these tools effectively. Instead, they're meant to spark your interest and encourage further research, given the wealth of available resources.

Personally, I've chosen an active rest method involving moderate physical activity. Passive rest, like watching a good movie or reading a book, rarely provided me with quality recovery. Even reading was a somewhat active form of recovery for me because I often read books on business and educational topics, which I was eager to absorb. Reading fiction or simple novels might have been a better form of recovery, but I found it challenging to read for extended periods without getting distracted or falling asleep.

Sitting on the couch and watching television or playing

video games was not a viable option for me. Partly because I didn't have a couch in my apartment, and partly because I found it hypnotic and unproductive. There was one sci-fi series I followed for a while, but as it became increasingly absurd, I realized it wasn't helping me recover effectively. While watching it, time seemed to stand still, and I was completely absorbed, but afterward, I couldn't remember what I had watched, as if I had missed out on that time.

Some individuals may prefer movies and video games as their preferred method of recovery, and interestingly, some make a living from such activities. It's up to you to decide if passive forms of recovery work best for you and whether you notice any improvements. Recovery should positively influence your mind and body, making you fitter, healthier, and stronger.

The pitfall of simple activities like watching TV or playing video games is that they require minimal effort and can be tempting ways to pass the time. It's easier to lie on the couch for thirty minutes than to go for a walk or run outside, even though exercise has many benefits. The initial discomfort, sweating, and physical effort can deter motivation, and it's easy to make excuses for staying on the couch.

However, it's important to consider small lifestyle improvements that can enhance your overall quality of life. These small steps accumulate over time. For example, running just two kilometers once a week may seem insignificant in the short term, but over a year, it amounts to more than a hundred kilometers. Consistency in such activities leads to even greater progress.

Similarly, think about your food intake. Small changes over time can lead to significant improvements. For instance, if you consume 50g of sweets daily, that's 1.5kg in a month and 18kg in a year. While 50g may not seem like much, picturing 18kg can highlight the cumulative effect of small changes.

Your diet may not seem directly related to your recovery from high-stress environments, but it plays a crucial role in maintaining a healthy mind and body. You don't need to go to extremes, but being aware of its contribution to your overall well-being is important. Understanding how much energy you expend in activities like swimming or running can help you appreciate a chocolate bar in a different light.

In essence, it's about eating to live, not living to eat. Balancing elements like diet and exercise in your daily routine leaves a mark on your mental and physical well-being. It becomes a signature that others can recognize, indicating that you're taking good care of yourself. It reflects self-discipline and confidence because a healthy lifestyle requires continuous effort and dedication, not just a one-time task to check off your to-do list.

One seemingly simple yet crucial aspect of a fulfilling life is having a hobby. Surprisingly, not everyone has one. While many are enthusiastic consumers of information on various topics, a hobby goes beyond this. It's an activity you engage in regularly during your free time, driven by passion and enjoyment.

Your chosen hobby can be both energizing and financially demanding. Regardless of its cost, it should naturally fit into your lifestyle. The purpose of a hobby is to direct your leisure time and recovery energy toward a well-defined, ideally smart, and measurable goal. Since a hobby is something you do for pleasure, it's understood that you want to excel at it and be well-informed and competent.

During the 2020 COVID-19 pandemic, I observed how important hobbies are. While spending time at the lake, I noticed people enjoying various activities like sailing, painting, biking, and more. They all took good care of their hobbies—well-used but well-maintained bikes, high-quality but not brand-new painting tools, and joyful boat riders. Regardless of their choice, you could see satisfaction and joy in their eyes as they dedicated time to activities they'd dreamed of doing for years. Their passions were already there, and now they had the time to pursue them wholeheartedly.

On the other hand, some people panicked during the pandemic. Suddenly, their jobs didn't demand their full attention, and they had too much time and uncertainty. They questioned their career choices, worried about financial security, and struggled to find ways to occupy themselves. Those with hobbies faced similar insecurities and doubts. They, too, were uncertain about their careers and income. However, some handled the situation better. They channeled their energy constructively into their hobbies and made the most of the situation.

Opportunities arose for everyone, but not everyone seized them. I knew two friends, both dentists. One lost confidence and feared losing patients, while the other, who was passionate about his profession, saw an opportunity to help others. He equipped himself with the necessary safety measures and announced that they were accepting patients needing urgent care. It was a positive message that resonated with people, and it brought him new customers and positive publicity. Both started from the same point, but their reactions to the crisis determined their outcomes.

This is why I believe having a hobby is essential for success. Successful individuals often indulge in their hobbies during their free time. It's not about the cost; it's about the consistency, passion, and dedication. In the long run, it brings benefits that might not be immediately apparent. Keep going and do it for your own sake and pleasure.

As individuals, we often feel the urge to accomplish everything quickly and independently. We strive for financial security and self-sufficiency. This can be draining because our time is limited. However, the companies we build are meant to outlive us and achieve results beyond our individual capabilities. Take the time to build your company correctly, with an emphasis on long-term sustainability. We tend to overestimate short-term achievements and underestimate what can be accomplished in the long run. Aim for the long term and prioritize your recovery to make the best decisions for your company's lasting success.

7.
A WORKING PRODUCT IS NOT A WORKING COMPANY

Initially, the team and the idea may have come together, but it could have been the other way around. Eventually, the product emerged – starting as a minimum viable version and going through numerous iterations until it reached a market-ready stage. In the early days of a startup, there's immense pressure and high expectations to create the first product or demo. It's crucial to have something to show to customers or potential investors. The team has learned various methodologies to optimize product development, including Agile methods, lean startup, and design thinking. These approaches all share a common goal: building a product quickly and efficiently to solve a well-defined customer problem. This underscores the product's importance for a new company.

For a company to generate substantial revenue, it must have a product to offer customers. In this chapter, when we refer to "product," we mean it in a broad sense – it could be a physical product, intellectual property, technology, or the foundational framework for an innovative business model. In most cases, money has to be invested in product development before any revenue is earned from the product. This phase is critical for finding the right product fit and identifying the fine line between a working prototype and a marketable product. It might take just a few days to create the first product, or it could involve several years of complex technological progress to reach the final product. Having the right team that possesses patience, a results-oriented mindset, and the ability to recognize and seize opportunities is crucial for successful product development, as very few get it right the first time.

A sort of impasse occurs when the business team demands a working product to sell while the product team needs clear requirements, more resources, and time to meet those requirements. As business requirements grow and change, more resources are allocated to product development. The technical team expands and adds more features to the product. The business team is pleased to see the product evolve until, at some point, they decide that it has enough features to begin commercialization.

This is a pivotal moment for the company as the product gets a clear version number or has the "beta" label removed from its title. The product works and includes most of the required features for the customer value proposition. At this stage of the company's evolution, most resources and energy have gone into the product. The technical team often outnumbers other departments within the startup, to the extent that functions like marketing and communication may be handled by non-experts to save costs that can be invested in the product. Business team requirements are diligently implemented, sometimes even against the advice of the technical team. In some rare cases, this approach leads to success, but in most cases, it negatively impacts team dynamics. Talented engineers, designers, or architects follow the lead of a confident but mediocre business leader whose vision may not be grounded in reality. Technological innovation is limited by implementing a rigid business vision, often developed from mediocre thinking and unreliable business reports. This is the opposite of times when microprocessors and space technologies were developed as a result of true technological evolution, allowing business cases to naturally emerge around the new technology.

With a reliable working product that meets the business specifications, the company's initiatives can now begin. They have acquired a few pilot customers who are using the product, and the feedback has been positive. The product is stable, and gone are the days when engineers had to reset databases and servers after every demonstration or apply midnight patches for early morning demos. There are no more sudden crashes with every action taken; the product is indeed working. This marks the start of a new phase, where existing features will mature, and new complementary features will be added.

However, despite the functionality of the product, the company finds itself facing challenges. The growth rate isn't skyrocketing, despite the positive feedback. The sales pipeline is weak, and the conversion rate of pilot customers to paying customers is low. Customer projects are small and limited to certain product features. The business team believes that adding more features will address the weak sales pipeline, but it's becoming clear that having a functional product is not the same as having a successful company.

Product management and development are just one part of the toolbox that founders can utilize. While they are essential, they are not the only tools available. Marketing, sales, human resources, and support are equally important aspects of building a successful company. These functions need to be balanced, and founders should utilize all the tools at their disposal to make the company thrive.

Sometimes, founders might overemphasize the importance of the product and neglect other functions. They may assume roles in requirements, marketing, sales, and support alongside their primary responsibilities. This could be due to financial constraints, delegation issues, or a desire to handle everything themselves. Regardless of the reason, it's not an excuse to neglect these functions; they are all crucial.

Marketing and communication are essential to make the public aware of your product. It's vital to present the product in a simple and understandable manner to potential customers. Human resources is crucial to taking care of your employees, who are your most valuable assets. Support functions are vital to keeping your customers satisfied. When pursuing large contracts with major corporations, having a great product is just one part of the equation. The big customers want to be reassured that there are enough resources to address their questions and provide support. While a great product is a strong asset, winning the game requires having other strong cards in your hand. Your customers and competitors will sense if you have a strong product but lack operational execution power, and this could work against your goals. The message you convey must be comprehensive: a great product, a clear vision, excellent support, and a strong company.

The line between promoting a product effectively and coming across as overconfident without substantial evidence is quite delicate. This is a common pitfall in the sales process, especially for sales and business leaders deeply involved in product development. They tend to overemphasize the future, promising that the next iteration will be even better, no matter how many features the current product already has. While it's generally true that product evolution should be positive, constantly highlighting future features and selling these improvements can negatively impact your sales pipeline.

Firstly, customers may perceive the product as incomplete and immature, expecting new features in future versions. Secondly, they might delay their purchase, waiting for the next version with more features to be released. This psychological effect can lead to a sales pipeline filled with prospects on hold and few closed sales. So, when is a product truly ready? It's ready when it provides added value to your identified customers at its current development stage. Once this decision is made, act as if you have the best solution available, be proud of your achievement, and demonstrate how your product can solve their problems.

A robust marketing and communications department can help counter this trend. They can position the product effectively in the right markets and emphasize its existing features. They remain closely connected to product development while maintaining a strategic distance to avoid becoming too enamored with new features. Professional, ongoing communication about your product and company's evolution is crucial. It represents your company to the industry and customers, just like bringing sound and color to silent movies enriches the experience. Focusing solely on product development and neglecting other organizational aspects can limit your company's ability to communicate its strengths effectively.

Similarly, other departments contribute to the perceived added value. A dedicated support team can serve customers better than founders managing issues with the help of engineers. Clear user documentation benefits from dedicated personnel rather than rushed efforts by a founder between sales meetings. Human resources departments are more effective at screening candidates and conducting targeted headhunting. Founders may be tempted to handle these tasks themselves and dedicate all resources to product development. While it's true that people can do many things, time is limited. You must decide how to allocate your time and resources, where to trust your team, and where to grow.

The goal should be to create a self-sufficient company that operates without central authority, i.e., you controlling every aspect of development. A scalable company with distributed tasks among members is more likely to succeed than a one-person show. Founders must learn to trust and delegate tasks to their teams, being content with limited control. You must carefully choose which tools to use and then entrust them to skilled team members. Relying solely on one tool, like excessive focus on product development, can lead to successes in some areas but indifference or damage in others. Balancing your toolkit with appropriate tools for different situations is the best long-term approach.

To build a successful company, you need to use the available tools to establish the right structure. It's essential that customers fully understand what they're buying and how it addresses their problems. You should also make it clear how your company generates revenue and how business needs translate into product features. As the founder, it's your responsibility to create a sustainable business structure capable of achieving more than you can do alone. In the early stages, you might wear multiple hats due to limited resources, which is normal. However, you should aim to acquire the necessary business tools as soon as possible.

Failing to allocate resources, believing that the product will sell itself once it's ready, is a fast track to failure. Your overall vision for the company must align with your growth strategy. If you choose to run a one-person operation, that's fine, but your expectations should match. For example, a single consultant can't expect to handle multimillion-dollar projects for large corporations without the necessary structure in place.

It's crucial to create a self-sufficient organization capable of handling projects and potential growth. Overinvesting in technical departments for a product that doesn't sell is wasteful. Similarly, attempting to manage larger projects with the same or fewer resources, without proper preparation, is impractical. Ensure you have the appropriate structures in place for a successful business.

Remember that starting a business is not the same as getting a regular job. The risks and rewards are higher. You've chosen to move beyond employment and create a business. Your role as a founder or project manager is to provide the necessary resources and information to your teams, not to have a fixed 9-to-5 job description. You should view your company as a business with secure revenue streams and value generation for shareholders. To succeed, you must assemble the right team, develop the right product, and bring it to market successfully. Your team should take ownership of their work, recognize opportunities, adapt to changes, and operate independently without constant supervision. Trust between you and your team is crucial, as a culture of fear hinders growth and scalability.

Many people believe that working long hours, day and night, weekdays and weekends, is the norm for founders and employees of startups. They often work tirelessly for below-market pay, all while hoping for significant financial rewards when the company succeeds. It's fascinating how much people are willing to sacrifice for the joy of their work and their belief in a meaningful cause.

To the startup's leadership team, asking employees to work more than their regular hours might seem like a simple way to reduce costs and increase productivity. On the surface, it appears to be a straightforward equation for success. However, in the long run, employees working at 150% capacity start to experience fatigue, lose motivation, and become less productive.

From a strategic perspective, pushing employees to constantly work beyond their limits is not a sustainable approach. While the team might be willing to go the extra mile repeatedly, maintaining such a high workload leaves no room for taking on new tasks or seizing new opportunities. The team may continue to work hard but will only be able to maintain their existing tasks without the energy to consider process improvements or optimizations.

Furthermore, such a high workload is detrimental to creativity, as it's often in moments of downtime that individuals come up with innovative ideas. In the long run, this approach can backfire, leading to a lack of growth capacity.

The negative effects can become evident when taking on new projects with larger customers. Even if a project bid is successful, there may not be enough resources available to meet quality standards, or resources will have to be shifted from other projects, causing resource shortages elsewhere.

Another scenario is when preparing for an exit, such as an acquisition by another company. During due diligence, the acquirer thoroughly evaluates the startup's workload, open tasks, customer project sizes, roadmaps, and team size. An overloaded team signals to the acquirer that the startup may not have the capacity to handle the merger and execute associated tasks while maintaining pre-merger growth levels.

While it may be tempting for founders to constantly push for a workload exceeding 100% to cut costs and increase short-term output, the hidden costs only become apparent in later stages when growth is hindered.

Cost cutting is a common practice in both startups and corporate settings. It's prudent to manage expenses efficiently and avoid unnecessary spending. However, some individuals take cost-cutting to an extreme, treating it like an art form where every euro is meticulously accounted for and optimization methods are obsessively pursued.

For instance, I once had a recurring argument with my partners about the cleaning costs for our Munich office. The office was a small space for six employees, and at times, I was the only one there or had just one colleague with me. The cleaning cost was less than €30 per month, yet my partners insisted I cancel the contract and handle the cleaning myself. I had done the cleaning myself in the early days of the company but refused to cancel the contract in the fifth year of operation.

My reasoning was that for a five-year-old company focused on customer acquisition, the success or failure shouldn't hinge on a €30 cleaning contract. If such a small expense could make or break the company, there were likely more fundamental issues with our business strategy.

This brings us to a critical issue with the cost-cutting approach as a guiding philosophy: eventually, it hits rock bottom. There's a limit to how much you can cut costs before you reach a threshold where further reductions are no longer feasible. For example, a software start-up can't function without laptops or internet access, a shipping company relies on logistics, and a bakery needs flour. The lowest point of cost-cutting is when it forces a business to shut down because it can't operate with any fewer resources. However, this shouldn't be the founder's ultimate goal. Relying on extreme cost-cutting as the core philosophy for a company is detrimental.

On the flip side, we have investing. Investing isn't incompatible with cost-cutting and expense management; they can coexist. Embracing a philosophy of investing in revenue growth and customer satisfaction is healthier for the company and team spirit. Unlike cost-cutting, revenue growth has no limits. A company can continually explore new products and services to increase its revenue streams. This philosophy encourages creativity within the team, pushing them to identify opportunities for revenue growth. The beauty of this approach is that there are no boundaries to what can be achieved—it focuses the team's energies on a goal beyond the current state and keeps them open to new possibilities. This philosophy thrives on limitless potential, starting from the status quo. In contrast, cost-cutting begins at the status quo and considers options for reducing operations and cutting services.

One tool highly recommended for founders is the pivot concept, popularized by Eric Ries in the Lean Startup model. It involves making significant adjustments to the company's strategy while maintaining the same overarching vision to steer the company toward success. There are ample resources available on the internet and in print for those interested in delving further into this topic. I mention this tool for those who may be unfamiliar with it and wish to add it to their toolkit.

Another highly effective but not immediately obvious tool, especially in the early stages of a startup, is portfolio diversification. It may not be apparent because startups often begin with a single captivating idea pursued by the founders. They work on executing their idea and transforming it into a viable business model. The initial idea becomes a marketable product or service, generating revenue. At this point, the team can concentrate on enhancing the product, adding new features, and scaling it. However, an equally important goal should be diversifying the product and service offerings.

Once a product reaches a market-ready state, founders should ensure that it has its own dedicated team capable of overseeing it independently, reducing the need for the founders' full-time attention. With one product operating somewhat independently, the founders can redirect their energy toward expanding the company beyond its initial offering, potentially creating second or third revenue streams. Diversification helps mitigate the risks associated with relying solely on one product and safeguards the company against significant market changes affecting that single product.

A successful global business requires a diverse range of products. Initially, having one scalable product is crucial for success, as it demonstrates effective management and delivery capabilities. This early success provides a strong foundation for future growth, and the cornerstone of this growth is product diversification. Continuously releasing new product versions and iterations is beneficial, as it allows flexibility to adapt to rapidly changing market demands. However, having a working product alone doesn't make a company successful. To ensure success, the company needs well-developed structures around each product in its portfolio. These structures should enable scalability and contribute positively to the company's financial health.

Even if a product is of high quality, backed by a capable team, and receives excellent customer feedback, it may not prove to be a sustainable business case. Factors such as unfavorable economies of scale, pricing that exceeds what customers are willing to pay, an immature market, or other reasons can hinder sustainability. It's essential to understand that in such cases, it's not the founder's failure but a mismatch between expectations and reality.

As a founder, you have tools at your disposal to improve the situation, but sometimes, especially in a single-product company, there may be limited options. For instance, consider free-floating car-sharing companies that offer a solid product and quality services. They have a healthy customer base and good utilization of their cars but struggle to turn a profit. This could be due to underestimating operational expenses in the initial business plan or customers being unwilling to pay higher prices that would offset individual automobile acquisition costs. Market predictions made years ago might not have materialized as expected.

In such cases, it's crucial to acknowledge that despite launching a good product with the right tools at the right time and executing well, the company may still face challenges in achieving profitability. As a founder, stay vigilant about your business case and be prepared to adjust your long-term strategy.

Communication is a tool that often goes unnoticed and is taken for granted. Only a few people truly excel in mastering their communication skills. In the next section, we will delve deeper into the importance of communication as a tool, as it is frequently underestimated by managers.

8.

THE ROLE OF COMMUNICATION

Communication is the process of sharing ideas and messages between people using a common language or symbols. When you want to communicate something to others, you first create the message in your mind and structure it in a way that makes sense to your audience. This message is then expressed through speech, text, or symbols and sent to the intended recipients. On the receiving end, the recipients decode the message and try to understand its meaning.

Although communication seems straightforward, it's fraught with complexities that often lead to misunderstandings and conflicts. For instance, technical issues can disrupt the transmission of messages, such as emails not reaching their intended recipients or conversations being overheard. Additionally, there are no strict rules for interpreting messages, so different individuals may understand the same message differently. In fact, sending the exact same email to two different people can elicit completely opposite reactions due to their subjective interpretations.

Effective communication is vital for founders and managers. While there's a wealth of information available on this topic, I want to stress its importance in this section. Communication is a valuable tool in your personal toolkit that should not be underestimated.

One key lesson I've learned is that you can't overcommunicate, especially in challenging times. Consistent and appropriate communication can make the difference between a company that survives and one that fails. Regardless of the content of your message, it's crucial to ensure that your entire team is on the same page. This fosters transparency and engagement among your employees, allowing you and your team to connect during both good and tough times. Overcommunication involves sharing messages frequently, which can range from multiple times a day to once a day or once a week, depending on the context. You have the flexibility to decide how transparent you want to be, but remember that frequent communication doesn't necessarily mean revealing every detail of your company's operations to every team member.

In our team, we established a daily call inspired by the Scrum meetings in agile development. This was necessary because we were working remotely from different locations. The call took place at the same time every day, and it served as a quick update on the work done the previous day and the tasks planned for today. Usually, these calls were quite short because there weren't usually major changes overnight. Often, we found ourselves discussing the same tasks as the day before. However, this daily call was essential to me for more than just sharing information; it had a social aspect. It allowed the team to come together, check in with each other, engage in a brief chat before diving into work, ensure everyone was aligned with our goals, and anticipate potential issues. Despite initial doubts about its usefulness, especially when there didn't seem to be much new information to share (an example of overcommunication), it proved valuable for keeping the team connected, which is crucial for remote teams, especially with the rise of remote work.

On the contrary, during the merger and acquisition process of the company, we experienced an opposite problem: under-communication. This happened before we received the letter of interest. In the early stages of an M&A process, both parties are getting to know each other and deciding whether to proceed with the acquisition. This process involves numerous internal and external stakeholders, each with a specific role in closing the deal. However, communication was challenging in this situation. Messages between the involved parties lacked substance and were infrequent. Furthermore, these messages were slow to reach all stakeholders. This communication approach may have been a deliberate negotiation tactic by the acquiring company to exert pressure, but it wasn't the best way to build trust and work toward a mutually satisfying agreement. The consequences of this under-communication were frustration, doubt, and a lack of motivation. We tested our patience as we repeatedly heard that we would learn more next week, which became a running joke in our team.

In such situations, it's good practice to communicate even when there's no apparent new information to share. Doing so shows respect for your partners and demonstrates ownership of the topic. People should not always have to ask if there's anything new that can impact their work. Nonetheless, it's an individual's responsibility to seek the information needed to perform their tasks. In fast-paced, innovative environments, individuals may not even know what they don't know, making it challenging to ask the right questions. Information should flow freely in all directions: top-down and bottom-up. In a communication-starved environment, some individuals may retreat into a mindset of "what you see is all there is," acting only based on the information they have. People grow tired of constantly requesting information or feel that information is being withheld from them, which can be a tactic used by managers to assert power by keeping information exclusive.

I strongly oppose such tactics and believe in healthy, continuous communication among peers. Communication should happen even when it doesn't seem immediately necessary because it can lead to the discovery of insights and early issue resolution. The "what you see is all there is" mentality is a self-preservation mechanism that limits an individual's development and innovation potential when there's more information that they don't have access to.

Always start your communication with facts. This helps your counterpart understand your position and the context. By doing so, you not only convey your preparedness but also earn the trust of your peers, contributing to productive cooperation. Remember, it's not your job title but your ability to lead that truly matters. To become an effective leader, you must wield communication efficiently and wisely.

Effective communication means timing your messages appropriately. For example, if a meeting has been rescheduled, notify participants well in advance to ensure everyone can attend. Maintain a clear and respectful tone and rhythm in your communication, as how you say something often leaves a lasting impression. Think back to your school or university teachers; you probably don't remember specific math or grammar lessons, but you do recall their values and principles.

To establish yourself as a leader, embody your beliefs and convey them through clear, factual communication.

As a leader, always speak consistently about others, whether they're present or not. This reflects mutual respect for your colleagues and builds trust, reducing office gossip and politics. Teams built on these principles tend to have higher employee satisfaction, resulting in increased productivity and better service quality. As a founder or manager, taking care of your employees and aligning them with the company's vision leads to better customer care, higher customer satisfaction, and increased revenue. Effective communication sets the stage for this upward spiral to success with minimal effort.

Communication is paramount! Even when you have no updates, proactively involve your peers in the matter at hand. I once found myself in a complicated situation within a startup, blamed for not being involved in a project I thought was under another office's responsibility. The project had a defined scope, and I had no reason to intervene. Then, I learned unexpectedly that the project was taking a different path, just minutes before it started. This was a clear example of poor communication among peers.

Remember that what you don't say can be as significant as what you do say. Deliberate omissions of information are akin to white lies. For instance, consider renting an apartment and asking the landlord if there's a dishwasher. If the landlord says yes but doesn't mention that it's broken, it creates a problem. While technically the landlord didn't lie because they answered your question truthfully, in an ethical context, omitting this detail is considered deceptive.

In the business world, ethics may not always align with profits, and people may sleep well at night by being technically truthful while omitting crucial details. However, a more ethical stance would be to provide complete and honest information in your communication.

One of the positive aspects of life is that we get to choose how we approach our interactions with others. We can choose to be honest and transparent, or we can choose to pursue our own goals without concern for others. Our choices are influenced by factors like education, economics, and our social environment, but ultimately, we have the power within to decide which path to follow.

In society, you'll find both types of people—those who value transparency and honesty and those who prioritize their own interests. Both groups coexist and have their own ways of thriving. However, when it comes to business, it typically aligns more with the transparent and honest approach. People tend to do business with those who share their values and principles.

This distinction in behavior is like the opposite poles of a magnet: opposites repel, and similar traits attract. It's a pattern that continues through generations as individuals make choices about how they want to conduct themselves.

We've all been in situations where discussing a sensitive topic feels daunting. These conversations could be about something personal, confidential, or something we know the other person won't like or agree with. Such conversations tend to stay with us for a long time.

My preferred strategy in such situations is to address the issue head-on. Start with the facts, communicate clearly, maintain a respectful tone and pace, and show respect for the other person's perspective. Even if you need them to accept something difficult, such as your decision to leave, you can handle it with grace. You can also give them the opportunity to share their thoughts and actively listen to their point of view, even if you don't agree. Handling these tough conversations in a civilized and mature manner can maintain and enhance.

Another strategy, often used in sales, is the concept of "low-hanging fruit." This means tackling the simplest and easiest tasks or conversations first. It makes sense to start with the straightforward topics, leaving the more challenging ones for later. However, I'm not a big fan of this approach because it can lead to neglecting the most critical issue. People may feel shortchanged if all the easy matters are resolved before addressing the main topic, eroding trust and confidence. Still, it's up to each individual to decide which strategy works best for them. Sometimes, both approaches, addressing the big issue upfront and dealing with smaller matters later, may be appropriate in different circumstances.

Communication is a crucial soft skill, but we often overlook the importance of active listening. Many times, while someone is speaking, we're already formulating our response in our heads. This prevents us from truly engaging in active listening, where we should focus on being present in the conversation and understanding the speaker's perspective. Simply acknowledging with phrases like "I agree" or "I understand" isn't enough. It's like the message enters one ear, briefly searches for a brain to process it, and exits through the other ear. We should strive to be better listeners.

Instead of rushing to reply, take a moment to gather your thoughts and provide a thoughtful response. Active listening is as vital as effective communication but often less explored. I want to emphasize this aspect of communication and encourage you to educate yourself in this area. By doing so, you can significantly improve your communication and relationships.

In today's world, much communication happens online

or in writing, especially during the COVID-19 pandemic, limiting face-to-face interactions. In these environments, we miss out on many non-verbal cues that play a crucial role in understanding messages. Non-verbal cues include posture, tone, vocabulary, eye movements, hand gestures, appearance, and body language. People often form their attitudes and perceptions based on these cues. Be mindful of both the non-verbal cues you receive and those you express, but use them judiciously to avoid confusion.

For online communication, consider implementing standardized processes. Establishing clear communication standards can improve efficiency and ensure everyone is on the same page regarding how and when to provide input. Simple actions like using tags in email subjects to indicate the topic, confirming message receipt with a short reply, or setting guidelines for online meetings can make a significant difference. These small steps can enhance team communication, leading to higher satisfaction, increased productivity, and improved quality.

This section provides a brief overview of the vast topic of communication. Think of it as a quick tour through a massive museum where you get a glimpse of all the rooms without spending too much time in any of them. I'm not an expert in any particular room of this museum, but as a founder, I've stumbled into various rooms and admired the treasures within. Now that I'm aware of the museum and its rooms, I can intentionally return and delve deeper into the areas of interest through lectures, research, and education. This section is meant to serve as a starting point for your exploration of communication.

9.
MY PERSONAL JOURNEY

I began my journey with the startup company in Toulouse on October 1st, 2015, just one day after leaving my socially secure consulting job. Shortly after earning my Master's degree in Informatics, I decided to enter the world of consultancy. I was drawn by the promise of challenging and diverse work in a highly competitive environment. With great excitement, I started my new job, but the reality did not exceed my expectations as the projects were not as demanding as I had envisioned. Perhaps my youthful ambition sought rapid progress and intensity, and I wasn't ready to settle down just yet.

During my studies, I had taken courses in entrepreneurship and was intrigued by the idea of creating a product from scratch. One of these courses exposed me to the intersection of the medical and technical fields. Our professor arranged a visit to a hospital, where we observed doctors in their working environment, looking for ways to apply technical improvements to the medical sector. It was my first time in an operating theater, and the experience left a lasting impression. However, I hadn't yet found or formed a dedicated founding team to pursue entrepreneurial success. Deep down, perhaps I was afraid and doubted my ability to start a company.

After setting aside the idea of becoming a founder, an opportunity arose through a university job posting for a technical co-founder. Even now, as I reread the ad, the required skills were remarkably diverse, covering areas from IT security and network topology to 3D geometry, software architecture, server administration, and 3D printing file formats. I couldn't imagine anyone fitting all these criteria. The unique blend of skills required and the prospect of being a co-founder intrigued me, prompting me to apply. The discussions with the other co-founders went smoothly, and soon we began working together on the project. Our collaboration had its share of ups and downs over a period of more than five years. Looking back, joining a startup was my primary motivation for embarking on this path. Little did I know just how challenging the journey would be.

I was filled with excitement and determination to turn our project into a marketable product and establish a scalable and sustainable company. Fueled by this energy, the morning after leaving my consulting job, I boarded a plane bound for Toulouse to join the team for the acceleration phase of our project. Being part of the inaugural group in the corporate accelerator brought us great visibility and a touch of glamour. However, behind the scenes, the processes were still taking shape, and things were not running as smoothly as they would eventually. The learning curve was steep for both the startups and the accelerator and coaching teams. The atmosphere was friendly, and the startups, especially those from outside the corporation, were eager to promote collaboration and showcase their progress.

Before I relocated to Toulouse, our company had already brought on board its first junior software developer, B. He shared a strong commitment to our project's vision, and we had a great working relationship. Collaborating with him was a pleasure, as we easily aligned on our daily tasks. B. consistently made time to deliver results, which was crucial for our startup. Like all of us, he had given up the security of a well-paying job to be part of this startup adventure.

During this phase of the company, I was actively involved in coding for our projects. The first prototype was built based on the business requirements from the job ad. Subsequently, we embarked on a greenfield project, which we developed alongside B. It's largely thanks to his dedication and contributions that we were able to complete it in such a short time and with limited resources. This beta product was showcased to our initial prospects and investors, marking a significant milestone.

My time in Toulouse left me with many remarkable memories. In hindsight, I'm amazed at how we managed our day-to-day chores. With the help of my co-founders, I secured a room in a shared apartment for the duration of my stay. Three of us lived in that apartment, and I shared a wall with one of my partners, making it easy to hear between rooms. What made this living arrangement unique was the ever-changing dynamic. Over the six months I spent there, we never settled into a routine. There was always something new and different happening. Of course, we had our disagreements about responsibilities and cleanliness, but when it was time to have fun and party, everything was forgiven.

Unfortunately, my French language skills weren't sufficient for social conversations, and it was often challenging for me to interact with my roommates' guests. I was surprised to discover that many native French students in that part of the country had limited English skills, unlike my previous experiences with foreign students where language barriers were less of an issue. In Toulouse, aside from fellow foreigners, it was difficult to socialize without a strong command of French. This lack of social interaction was a downside of my stay, but I still cherished the opportunity to immerse myself in the local culture of the Toulouse area.

My social life mainly revolved around my French co-founders, and I was grateful to be included in their social circle. I have vivid memories of some parties, including one hosted by our accelerator coach. Most of our gossip and inside jokes originated from a local bar nearby, which seemed to be a never-ending source of surprises and interesting people.

During my time in Toulouse, I had the chance to learn the rules of rugby and even watched my first game. To my surprise, it wasn't as complex and brutal as I had imagined.

Unfortunately, my private and regular sports activities took a back seat during this period. In Germany, I used to bike and swim frequently, but swimming was less accessible in Toulouse, possibly due to transportation and cost constraints, and I lacked a proper bike. My partners and I borrowed bikes from a fellow building resident, despite their poor condition, to explore the city and the Canal du Midi. These bike rides provided a welcome break and an opportunity to explore the surroundings.

In addition to biking, I enjoyed many long walks in the city, admiring the distinctive architecture of red terracotta bricks and strolling along the banks of the Garonne River. These walks served as a form of retreat and recovery after challenging days at the startup, where I had to grapple with technical solutions and make decisions with far-reaching implications. Due to our financial limitations, with only a few exceptions, I didn't get to indulge in the exquisite treats of French cuisine.

However, we did manage to take trips to nearby cities and even had a memorable dinner at a renowned entrecote restaurant in Toulouse. One amusing memory stands out: we embarked on a bike trip to Castelnaudary with high hopes of savoring an authentic French cassoulet, as it's considered the birthplace of this famous dish. To our surprise, when we arrived, all the restaurants were closed for lunch. We couldn't find any appealing options until we stumbled upon a restaurant serving traditional Romanian dishes. So, three of us, hailing from France, Hong Kong, and Romania, biked to Castelnaudary with the intention of enjoying a classic cassoulet but ended up having a traditional Romanian lunch instead. It was an unexpected twist in our adventure, just one of many surprises I encountered during my time in Toulouse.

During my time in Toulouse, I had a mindset of living on a tight budget and trying to save money wherever possible. This led to some unexpected and interesting experiences, with one of them making me question current eating habits.

Firstly, we often ate at a nearby fast-food restaurant. Initially, it was because it was one of the few dining options within our budget, and secondly, it was conveniently close to our apartment. What surprised me was that having a meal at this well-known global fast-food chain was actually cheaper than buying groceries from the nearby supermarket and cooking at home. This raised questions about how eating habits in lower-income groups are affected by factors like the economy of scale. It's disheartening to realize that eating healthily and fresh isn't affordable for everyone.

On a lighter note, two other stories stand out. The first involves spending time at the accelerator, socializing with partners, and enjoying free food at events. Leftover food would be stored in a communal fridge, and in the days following these events, we'd scavenge the fridge for our meals. When we didn't have access to free food, our diet mainly consisted of microwaved frozen meals and biscuits.

The second story is more adventurous. We learned about a religious service for young people that concluded with a communal dinner, and despite some initial hesitation, two of us decided to attend after weeks of contemplating the idea. It was a memorable experience, and we checked off doing something different and exciting from our list.

Not all the social events we attended were centered around food. In my first week in Toulouse, I attended an innovation night organized by the corporate accelerator. There, I had the chance to explore the latest aerospace technology innovations. During the event, my accelerator coach recognized one of the attendees as a co-author of a well-known business strategy theory. We exchanged ideas, took a picture together, and even had the executive of the famous author approach us for a copy of the photo. Little did we know that this random encounter would shape the future of our startup. It was through this connection that we were introduced to the investors who would fund our company at an early stage.

Several months passed between the initial meeting and the closing of the investment deal. It was an incredibly exciting time. In the appendix, I've included a letter I wrote at the request of the investors outlining the company's vision for the next five years. You can feel the excitement in every word. Our founding team was thrilled and eager to take on the challenges that lay ahead. When the investment funds finally arrived in the company's account, it was a pivotal moment for us, as we had never seen so much money in one place before. The sight of all those zeros was impressive, but we remained committed to living frugally, avoiding unnecessary expenses whenever possible, and even cutting back on some essential ones.

With this investment, we planned to expand our technical team and invest in product development.

The initial acceleration phase was supposed to last for six months. After that, I returned to the company's roots in Munich to start the local office. The company had its beginnings at a Munich university, and the plan was to establish it there. However, our success with the corporate accelerator application in Toulouse led us to move there temporarily, while my partners settled in Toulouse and established the French headquarters. It might not have been their original plan, and Toulouse might not have been their dream city, but they made the move for the sake of the startup, which is something worth appreciating. We didn't discuss this topic in depth, but in hindsight, it was a good decision to be based in Toulouse. The Munich office made sense because it was close to many major industry providers that our startup would partner with.

After receiving investment based on the second software prototype, our goal was to expand the team with senior developers and industrialize our product offering.

Soon after, we hired S. as a senior full-stack engineer in Munich, and J. joined as a freelancer. B. remained a reliable part of our team. Together, we decided on the technical stack and architecture based on the existing prototype and the lessons we had learned in the previous months. This marked the third and final time we started the code from scratch. I was highly motivated, and the team was too. In just over six months, with S. playing a vital role due to his extensive development experience, we went from sketches on a flip chart to a product deployed in production, connected to five industrial machines. We were all proud of this achievement, and the successful stress tests in production brought relief. I remember we celebrated that evening with a special Toulousain entrecote.

With this initial commercial success, I was motivated to maintain a fast pace and grow the company. In Munich, we moved between three shared offices with other startups before finally settling into our own modern building, which provided enough space for six employees and potential for expansion. We handled the move ourselves and had fun doing it. The team worked well together, with S. and B. focusing on the back-end while J. managed the front-end. Communication was smooth, and progress was consistently recorded.

I took a results-oriented approach with the team, emphasizing the importance of delivering agreed-upon results on time rather than dictating when, how, and where they worked. This trust-based approach led to faster and higher-quality work. As they had freedom over their time, team members often committed code on weekends or late at night. There was even some activity on Christmas day, which was done willingly by the team members as they saw fit.

My personal highlight years were the second and third years after founding the company. During this time, the product roadmap was clear, the core team worked well together, and everything seemed to be on track. We organized adventurous team events like rafting on the Isar river, sledding near Munich with the Toulouse team, and attending Oktoberfest. The technical team in Munich continued to expand, and we hired young graduates through a French program to work from the German office. I have wonderful memories that go beyond business relations, such as sharing pizza at Massimo or deciding between soup and salad at the Greek place with E. and S.. P. joined the team later and he was the last one to leave the Munich office. P. is a very kind person with many interesting stories to tell from his experiences. Besides his front-end code contributions to the company, he was an important sounding board for discussing a variety of topics from skiing to sketching.

During the early stages of our venture, we recognized the importance of catering to our customer base in French-speaking countries. To achieve this, we expanded our technical team in these regions. It made perfect sense to have team members who could communicate with customers in their native language. Over time, we welcomed further colleagues who played a significant role in shaping our code base and improving our project's development operations.

Our close proximity to our business partners meant that communication channels were short and effective, which greatly facilitated our interactions. Together, we handled a wide range of topics in France and earned praise from our satisfied customers.

Aside from product development and team expansion, the second and third years after our company's founding provided me with valuable opportunities to represent our organization externally. I considered it a privilege to be invited as a startup guest or panel member to discuss topics related to additive manufacturing. These events varied in scale, ranging from global events like the Paris Air Show to smaller gatherings featuring key players from the European region.

It's worth noting that these events were not suitable for direct sales, as they primarily attracted top management and investors, but rather for relationship building, communication and visibility. When these events included startup competitions in some form, we often received recognition and prizes, though not always the top prize. Preparing for these events was both enjoyable and challenging. I often felt nervous because the attendees were experts in their respective fields. I questioned whether my language and message were appropriate and whether I, as a junior in the industry, could contribute meaningfully to the discussions.

Nonetheless, I was impressed by how open and eager people were to learn about new technologies. It was easy to connect with them, as we all recognized each other as humans beyond our professional roles.

These events were instrumental in my personal growth and our network expansion. They significantly boosted our startup's visibility and brand recognition. I firmly believe that intangible assets like reputation are vital for a growing company. With a strong reputation, supported by a robust product and sales pipeline, we gained access to highly qualified employees and investment opportunities, which were essential for our continued growth.

As a founder, I still believe one of your roles is to represent your company to external stakeholders and ensure its continuous growth. Regardless of your specific role within the founding team, you are, in the early days of a startup, its public face.

As our team had grown, we had senior developers on board, and I had stepped back from full-time coding myself. The reason for this was twofold. First, I felt that my skills were best suited for creating initial technology demonstrators, where I could work across a broad range of technologies without being an expert in any one of them. Second, this was precisely why I had formulated our strategy to hire experts in their respective fields: to equip them with the necessary tools to excel in coding while I concentrated on company growth.

I would empower a results-oriented work culture and remove any blockers for them to able to make individual decision. In this mindset, I would engage with the team to discuss deliverables and agree on the deadlines. I ensured they had all the necessary tools and information to meet their goals. The team had the autonomy to decide upon their working schedule. My expectation from the team was to respect deadlines, be aligned while my responsibility was to ensure there were no obstacles hindering their progress. My partners favored a stricter control approach. At one point they opposed the idea of remote work, believing it would lead to reduced productivity. The debate escalated when one colleague, who had been successfully working remotely for over a year, joined the Munich office full-time. Despite his consistent performance, remote work was not an option anymore.

As the company pursued a following round of fundraising, the market conditions had changed. In negotiations with a large corporation for investment, they proposed a 100% acquisition of our shares instead. Seeing this as a viable option for the company and its employees, we began the acquisition process. These negotiations extended for about six months without reaching a conclusion. In the meantime, we engaged with experts and professionals of mergers and acquisitions. After long negotiations, we entered into exclusivity with one potential acquirer. Everything seemed promising, with professional consultants supporting us and a positive due diligence process. Surprisingly, the buyer withdrew their offer after successful due diligence, prior to signing the final contract. This unexpected turn of events caught us by surprise, leaving both us and our advisors puzzled, as similar situations were extremely rare in their experience.

The situation took a dramatic turn, going from the best-case scenario to the worst in just a matter of hours. We received no clear explanation for why the offer was suddenly withdrawn, especially when it was public knowledge that no red flags had been identified during the audit. We were left completely bewildered.

Upon hearing the news, we had to take immediate action and reconsider our plans. Looking back is was a prompt reaction from the founders. Beyond the operational aspects, it was an emotionally challenging time. One of the most difficult moments during my time with the company was the call with the team right breaking the news – they took it surprisingly well.

Personally, this was an incredibly tough period for me. I was left wondering about my next steps and whether the work I had put into the company over the past five years would still have value. All these questions were unanswered, and I felt trapped in a situation without a clear direction, as my world seemed to crumble. Emotionally, I hit rock bottom. Unfortunately, such events tend to bring out the best and worst in people at the same time. My relationships with my business partners deteriorated, and communication became strained while the bond with my partner became stronger and stronger. While the company was eventually acquired in France, it was not the high-profile exit one would hope.

Did I always apply the lessons I've discussed in this book throughout this journey? The honest answer is no. In fact, I may not have applied them even in 50% of the situations. The question of "why" it happened as it did is not a productive one, as it pertains only to the past. When I embarked on this journey, I hoped to gain valuable insights and have life-changing experiences. Perhaps I should have wished for something different—a self-sustaining, growing business. However, I ended up gaining more experience than I could have ever imagined, both positive and negative. I pushed my patience to extreme levels of self-sacrifice, setting the bar for my living standards very low, which ultimately hurt not only me but also my close family and friends who witnessed my struggles.

Often, we hear of success stories where, after numerous sacrifices, a great reward awaits. However, I learned that no matter how many sacrifices you make, success is not guaranteed. Instead, it's crucial to take care of yourself, maintain a healthy balance in all aspects of your life, and set high standards while striving to live up to them. At one point, I was relieved that the story had come to an end, as I could no longer endure the uncertainty of waiting for something – the great exit - to happen. This holding pattern had persisted for nearly two years, and anyone in their right mind would have lost patience by then.

When I finally accepted that a successful acquisition wasn't in the cards, my entire world crumbled. I felt incredibly sad and depressed because all my plans depended on that outcome. But soon, I realized that the physical world around me hadn't changed one bit. People went about their business, nature continued its course with flowing waters, enduring mountains, and changing seasons. The years ticked by without a care. I learned a hard lesson: the only thing that had changed was the world inside my mind.

This inner world was like fiction, and I had full control over it. I could shape it and let it flow into the real world through my actions. It was within my power to imagine what I could become. When I initially started the company, it was all about gaining life-changing experiences. It turned out that my subconscious plans aligned perfectly with what I achieved, even though my vision statement for 2021 said something different. It felt like the entire universe conspired to give me what I wished for – an unforgettable experience.

On this journey, I made the bold decision to leave behind the secure and predictable world of corporate life I had seen growing up and embrace the call of adventure: starting my own business. I wasn't fully prepared, had many doubts, and even resisted the idea several times. However, with this start-up company, everything fell into place – the requirements, expectations, industry, knowledge, and my curiosity all aligned, pushing me to take the leap into entrepreneurship. Along the way, I faced numerous challenges, encountered both allies and adversaries, and discovered abilities within myself that I never knew existed. I experienced both suffering and immense joy.

As my first startup experience draws to a close, I find myself returning to my daily routine with a newfound sense of contentment and happiness in life's small pleasures. The lessons I've shared in the previous chapters are like a source of strength for me, a magical elixir that will fortify me in future situations. Perhaps the most important lesson I've learned is that anyone can achieve what they dream of if they have a deep desire and belief in themselves. Would I do it all over again? I eagerly look forward to the opportunity. Only this time, I'll shape a different world in my mind – one filled with abundance, success, satisfaction, and boundless joy.

10.
APPENDIX

Letter dated 21.04.2016, on the TGV train between Paris and Munich

The Year 2021

our startup is an established trademark in the aerospace, automotive, maritime and digital factory industry. Our offices around the world provide our customers with the same quality products and support we offered since our first days when we were a young start-up of 3. Today millions of file transactions are processed per second through our software while driving the majority of industrial 3D printers across the globe. Our patented data distribution technology is the backbone of the modern digital supply chain for 3D printing. We enable a digital world where everything from the initial design to the final deliverable is linked and its availability for the entire product life time is ensured. Our customers are connected in real-time to their production units and discover detailed insights through our advanced data analytics algorithms.

To achieve this vision we have to build today a framework and a company that drives profitable growth. This growth can be achieved by keeping up with the work we have done until now, always challenging the status-quo and never take anything for granted. We build today trustworthy and personal relationships with the major players in their industry, from 3D printer manufacturers to high-tech corporations. The trust we are building is placing very high expectations on the product quality we provide, yet it is exactly the quality of our products which enables an exponential growth. We provide a solution to a pin-pointing customer problem, may it be loss of millions of dollars due to inappropriate handling of 3D printing data, a lack of digitalized tracking of the quality of the printed parts or a missing integrated software platform to monitor 3D printer production across the globe. Our growth is generated by continuously improving our products. For this we listen carefully to our customers and spice-up their requirements with our expertise. In this line of thought, we maintain our originality and provide solutions that save time, money, and make complex transactions seem easy. To keep a high growth rate we have to grow our selfs ahead of the market by taking action where others stand still.

There are many open questions in today's 3D printing industry, yet despite our daring dreams we have to start small and tackle challenges one after another. The focus now is to close the financing round and then direct our energy towards the technical & commercial development of our product. The top priority on the commercial side is to build the trust relationships with 3D printer manufacturers to gain access to their APIs. In the same time we are driving forward the collaboration with the corporate accelerator to have two pilot projects running within their premises and handle the internal 3D printing production between the different sites. One proof of concept should start with the ground support equipment depart- ment and the second with the ALM platform. Having the large corporation as a pilot customer is in itself a tremendous achievement for a start-up, however we are pushing further: Once we have managed the international production we envision to handle the external production. The goal here is to drive all the industrial printers through our software: at first all 3D printers of a printshop on one site and then extend to a second, geographically remote location.

Achieving all the above requires a lot of technical effort. For this reason we are looking to grow our technical team. Finding the right team is a long endeavor for a young start-up, nonetheless it is a crucial activity. Beyond the right technical capabilities we are screening candidates that prove a strong commitment to our cause and believe with all their heart in our vision. We are looking for the right combination between commitment, technical skills and star character. The stars do not fit one-to-one with the open job description but own the brain power to learn them quickly. This will prove a competitive advantage when we will be facing new, unexpected challenges as they have the power and creativity to approach the issues in a unique manner.

On a personal note, following a product from its initial phase on the drawing board to the customer service is highly challenging but brings enormous satisfaction having a happy customer. Intuition, knowledge, people skills and the right team to do the job right are required to bridge two worlds: the business and technical one. I am delighted by the moments of satisfaction when I do things right, yet many wrong steps are taken, many get disappointed and many people quit. I strongly believe, the real game changers are the ones who stand up and get back on the line. They have learned what they have done wrong and know, how to do the right step right next time in order to move the world towards a better future. And this is what I want to do for 3D printing: build the company to make a better future!

ABOUT THE AUTHOR

Andrei Mituca is a software engineer and entrepreneur born in Transylvania, blending the best of Romanian and Saxon cultures. After making a move to Germany, he took on the entrepreneur hat, lighting up his team with his clever ideas and upbeat spirit. They achieved some amazing things together! Always on the lookout for the next big tech thing, Andrei's enthusiasm has shaped some top-notch products and brought together fantastic international teams.